Riding with

JEB STUART

Riding with

JEB STUART

Hunting Adventures with an English Pointer

GEOFFREY
NORMAN

THE LYONS PRESS

Guilford, Connecticut
An imprint of The Globe Pequot Press

The Lyons Press is an imprint of The Globe Pequot Press.

10 9 8 7 6 5 4 3 2 1

Printed in the United States of America

Library of Congress Cataloging-in-Publication Data

Norman, Geoffrey.
  Riding with Jeb Stuart : hunting adventures with an English pointer / Geoffrey Norman.
    p. cm.
  ISBN 1-59228-228-8 (trade cloth)
  1. Pointer (Dog breed)--United States--Biography. 2. Bird dogs--United States--Biography. 3. Norman, Geoffrey. I. Title.
SF429.P7N67 2005
636.752'5--dc22
                         2005022540

To the ladies in Jeb's life—
Marsha, Brooke, & Hadley.

Riding with

JEB STUART

ONE

We had been driving for two days, and by the time we got where we were going, we had traveled more than sixteen hundred miles. By eyeballing the map, I figured we were almost exactly in the middle of the lower forty-eight. The town was Halsey, Nebraska.

"Well," I said, "we made it."

There was only one motel in town. A little, one-story building with white siding and a small sign out front where I parked and eased out from under the wheel, stiff from all the driving. The air was cold and there was a sharp wind. Out here in the plains, where there are no city lights, you can see hundreds of bright stars on a clear night. But when I looked up, I saw only three or four; dim and yellow, through the gathering clouds.

It was warm in the little motel office. The woman had been expecting me and had the key ready.

"Getting cold out there, isn't it?" she said. There was a television on in the room behind her. She was watching *Law & Order*. One of the hundreds of episodes in rerun.

"Sure is," I said.

"Might be bringing some snow down from Canada."

"Feels like it."

I wrote my name, address, and license number on the form and gave her my credit card. She was about to run it when I noticed the little sign behind the desk.

RATE: $39.00. DOGS: $10.00 EXTRA.

"I do have a dog," I said.

The woman nodded, made a change on the form, ran the card, then handed me the key.

"Thank you," I said. "And good night."

"Good night," she said, and went back to her show.

I went back outside and opened the hatch on the little SUV.

"Good news, Jeb," I said. "Tonight, you sleep on the bed."

Before I unpacked and inspected our quarters, Jeb and I took a walk along the street that ran in front of the motel, down to a train crossing, and off into the empty prairie. Jeb seemed as relieved to be out of the wagon as I was. He had spent a long two days, curled up in the passenger seat or in back, on top of my duffel. We had pulled in at a couple of dozen different rest stops on the interstate where he would smell the bushes and do his business, and I'd give him some water and then we'd load up and press on. We had spent last night in my daughter's small, student apartment on the South Side of Chicago. We'd walked a couple of blocks from the lot where we'd parked and that had been more or less the sum of Jeb's exercise for two full days. This was just about insupportable, especially at this time of year. It was fall, and that meant bird season. Jeb was born to run and hunt birds.

So I walked on out the road, beyond the railroad crossing, to give Jeb a chance to stretch his legs. He ran ahead of me but I could make him out in the darkness by the white on his coat. He moved from one side of the road to the other, occasionally checking back in my direction or stopping to investigate some compelling smell and then raising his leg to mark the offending spot. It might have been new territory, but that didn't mean it wasn't *his* territory.

Jeb was leaving a message along both sides of the road. "Okay, boys. New sheriff in town."

After about twenty minutes, my nose was cold, and without gloves, my fingers were getting stiff. I was ready to turn around and get established in our new quarters, but Jeb could have gone for another hour, another five miles. Unlike the streets and sidewalks on the South Side of Chicago, which had confused him and made him nervous, this was fine running country. A dog could learn to love it here . . . wherever *here* was. And, I imagined, to Jeb's mind, it didn't make much difference. Here . . . there . . . as long as a dog could ramble and work some scent.

I turned back and whistled for him.

"Come on, man."

I'd made twenty or thirty steps in the other direction when Jeb came highballing past me, running hard, like he had just been warming up before and had now truly hit his stride.

"Jeb . . . *here*."

That turned him, and he came back to me and stood at the side of my leg, panting and wagging his tail. I ran my hand down his flank to calm him.

"Easy, bud. Easy."

Running could seem intoxicating for him sometimes.

"Easy, my man. You won't believe how much running you'll get to do the next few days."

This, of course, made no impression on him, and he quivered, waiting for me to release him.

I slapped him, lightly, on his haunch, and that was the signal. He was off again, like a racehorse, breaking clean from the gate. He ran like that when he wasn't hunting; when he was running for just the sheer, exuberant hell of it.

"That dog of yours," a bird-hunting companion had once said to me, "he sure does like to see the ground go rolling under his belly."

"You don't know the half of it," I said.

◆

When we got back to the motel, I unloaded the wagon and filled Jeb's dish and put it on the floor. He ate while I unpacked and laid things out for the morning. Boots, briarproof pants, hunting vest, shells . . . shotgun. I ran down the mental checklist. I had already picked up a license in the last town big enough to support a Wal-Mart.

When everything was ready, I thought about calling home and telling my wife that we had arrived safely, but it was late back on the East Coast and I didn't want to wake her. So I set an alarm and got under the covers. Jeb finished his supper and went into the bathroom where he drank from the toilet. Bad habit, and one of many I hadn't been able to break him of. At least he never went thirsty.

I had the light on and was reading when he came back out and curled up on the floor, close to the heater.

"Hey, man. You can get up here." I patted the empty side of the bed.

Jeb looked at me. I had managed to train him not to get up on the bed at home.

"It's okay, bud—I paid the extra ten bucks. You're legal."

Another long stare.

"Come on, Jeb. Kennel up."

It wasn't exactly the right command. It was the one I used when I wanted him to climb aboard whatever vehicle I was driving. But since I didn't have a command for "Get on the bed," it seemed like the next best thing.

Jeb wasn't buying. Funny, I thought, how some dogs will choose which rules to honor and which to ignore—and when. It was plain to me that he understood what I wanted him to do, but he wasn't going to let me off easy. I had told him, over and over, not to get up on the bed at home. This was payback. If I wanted him up on the bed with me, well, then, I was going to have to beg.

"Come on, bud."

The stare.

"Jeb. *Kennel up.*"

No dice.

I finally had to get up and lift him onto the bed. Once he was there, he promptly curled himself up, settled in at my feet, sighed, and closed his eyes. The way I read him—body language and such—he was coming around a bit, after those long two days on the road. He'd been able to run a little—not enough by a long stretch—but that might change to-morrow, and he'd been fed, and now he'd even played some mind games with the Man (that would be me) and won them. Furthermore, he was sleeping on a nice, soft bed instead of the hard, cold floor. All in all, not too bad. A dog could live with that.

And I was probably as content, in my way, as he was in his. This was a trip I had wanted to make for a very long time. Since Jeb was a puppy, and probably for a long time before that.

I turned out the light and went to sleep, thinking of big country and pointed birds.

TWO

My partnership with Jeb went back ten years, to a pretty morning in July when my daughter Brooke and I were out running for exercise. She was fifteen and on the cross-country team at school, so she had the wind to talk while we ran.

"Dad," she said, "do you think you'll ever get another dog?"

It wasn't the hardest question she could have asked. There were many possibilities I would have dreaded a lot more. Still, I couldn't come up with an easy answer.

"I don't know," I said. "Maybe." It was an evasion, but then, she was used to that.

It was, in fact, time for a new dog, but I was stalling. I'd had a good, long run with my first bird dog, a Brittany named Molly, but now she was over the hill, too old and crippled to do much but sleep all day and eat when I fed her. She was way too arthritic to run. Merely walking across the room to the food bowl was an ordeal, and some nights she wasn't even up to that. I should have already been breaking in a new dog for a season or two now. But . . . there was something paradoxically final about getting a new dog. It would be as much an ending as a beginning, and I didn't want to face that. You can think you are all hard-nosed, but dogs will inevitably bring out the softie in you.

My neighbor Andy, who was the best and most serious bird hunter I knew, had already been through the same thing. He had hunted for years with a strong, exceedingly capable Brittany named Ruff. (There was a second Brittany, for a while, and this partner was called Ready. But that dog had died prematurely.) One of the most widely accepted theories when it comes to bird dogs is that the temperament of the dog should match that of the master, and this was undeniably the case with Ruff and Andy. They were both fiercely single-minded about bird hunting. They went out early and came home late. They hunted tough country and covered a lot of ground and did it thoroughly. They didn't walk the log roads and they didn't leave cripples in the brush. Hunting with them was serious business, and they didn't tolerate amateurs. It was ordinarily just the two of them because other hunters—and especially other dogs—usually didn't measure up. Lanny would shoot fifty or sixty grouse in a season when most other hunters in our area were happy to kill a dozen.

When Ruff began to run down and couldn't hunt the whole day any longer, Lanny had started talking about bringing another dog along. But he never made it past the talking. Then, one day, Ruff couldn't go at all, and Lanny simply quit hunting grouse altogether and started running beagles after snowshoe hare.

He went out with me a few times, when I invited him, and he said complimentary things about my dog. One evening, after we'd finished up and were back at the truck, he advised me to get a puppy a couple of years before my Molly began to visibly lose it. That had been his mistake, he said.

"You need to make a smooth transition," he said. "Otherwise, it's just too damned hard."

But I hadn't taken his advice. I wasn't in his class as a bird hunter, and Molly was not in Ruff's league as a bird dog; nonetheless, the pattern seemed to be holding. I was thinking I might not hunt birds any longer, now that Molly couldn't go in the field. I didn't have the heart.

(Molly only lasted another month. She died peacefully and I buried her in the backyard.)

"Don't you *want* another dog?" my daughter said. We'd run a half mile or so in silence since she'd first brought it up—me panting heavily while she seemed to be hardly breathing at all.

"Oh, I don't know," I said. Then, "Yeah, actually, I *do* want another dog. I just haven't gotten around to doing anything about it."

"Well, if you got one, what kind would it be?"

This was a question I could answer directly. No thinking and no evasions. "A pointer," I said.

"Not another Brittany?"

"No," I said. "I've always wanted a pointer."

I was panting too hard to explain it just then, but when we were back at the house, drinking water and cooling down, she asked again.

"Pointers," I said, "were what I grew up with. You said 'bird dog' and you meant just one thing—and that was *pointer*."

That had been in the South—Alabama, to be precise, in the southern part of the state, on the Florida line and the Gulf Coast—where hunting birds meant quail, and it was done with big, hard-going, and hardheaded pointers. Strong dogs with an unmistakable strain of hound in their breeding, they would work themselves bloody—literally—in the thick briars, looking for birds. To a young boy, there was something appealing, and a little thrilling, about their determination. They did not seem to require affection, like the house dogs I knew. They were stoics—aloof and even noble. You thought of those solitary cowboys in movie westerns. If John Ford had ever made a dog movie, then the best roles—the John Wayne and Ben Johnson parts—would have gone to pointers.

"Do pointers make good pets?" my daughter asked, skeptically.

"Back then, people didn't think so," I said. "Most of the men I knew who owned pointers kept them outside in kennels. There were even people who just chained them to a tree until it was time to go hunting. The dogs never came in the house."

She made a face. We'd bought Molly when my daughter was four. While she was my bird dog, Molly was also a pet. Brooke and her younger sister, Hadley, loved Molly and pampered her. There were a lot of mornings when we found her in one or the other girl's bed.

"I know," I said. "But it wasn't cruelty, exactly. People considered them working animals, like livestock, and you didn't bring the horses into the house, either."

"If you had a pointer," she said, "would you let him in the house?"

"Sure," I said. "You'd have to. A dog like that would freeze up here."

We lived in Vermont, where Brooke had been born. It had been a long time since I'd lived in the South, but I still thought of myself as a Southerner. My Vermont neighbors also thought of me that way. To them, I was a special breed of "flatlander."

"They're really Southern dogs," I added. "I don't know anyone who hunts one around here. In fact, I don't think I've ever seen one up here."

"Why do you want a pointer, then?"

I couldn't really explain why. The breed was wrong for the kind of hunting we did in Vermont, where you went into old apple orchards that had gone by or into tight aspen thickets. A good piece of cover might take up less than twenty acres of ground, and you could hunt it out in half an hour. You wanted a close working dog, which was why people like my neighbor Lanny settled on Brittanys, a French breed that was known, according to the legend, as the "poacher's dog." They worked close, with men who would sneak onto the great estates and take some of the noblemen's game. There was something furtive, even sneaky, about them.

Pointers, on the other hand, were entirely out front. They were "big-going dogs," and they liked to cover the country. In Texas and the plantation country of the South, hunters often rode horseback or followed along behind the dogs in jeeps or mule wagons. Even if you hunted on foot, the way I had when I was a boy, the dog was usually way out ahead and sometimes, literally, out of sight, making long casts through the broomweed and wire grass. It was in their nature to run.

Maybe, I thought, my desire to own a pointer was just a kind of nostalgia, as impractical as looking up the girl you'd taken to the prom. It seems like most people who leave the South eventually start to miss it. And pointers were among the best memories I had. Better, by far, than the prom.

"I can't really explain it," I said. "But, you know, I've heard that pointers can make good pets."

I'd also read that they could be trained to hunt close. Maybe not as tight as a Brittany, but close enough to work grouse and woodcock in the kind of country we hunted in Vermont.

"Would you get a male or a female?"

"Oh, a male, definitely."

"Why?"

Again, I wasn't sure. It just seemed right, somehow. The male dogs I remembered had more of the essential characteristics that I associated (in my romanticized memories) with bird dogs. The drive, the hard-headedness, the urge to hunt and keep hunting. If a pointer was an irrational choice for me—and, plainly, it was—then it seemed right to go all the way. The male of almost any species, it seems, is more irrational than the female.

"What would you name it?"

That was an easy one. I'd decided on the name even if I wasn't really serious about getting the dog.

"Jeb Stuart," I said.

The name didn't mean anything to her. I explained a little, but she didn't quite get it. She hadn't yet read about the Civil War in history class.

Brooke had, of course, been spying for her sister, Hadley, and their mother. I had a birthday coming up, and the three of them had decided to give me a puppy for a present. It was a decision that we would all come first to regret, and, eventually, to consider nothing short of in-spired. But that is getting ahead of the story.

Once my wife, Marsha, had the information she needed—namely, that the dog of my dreams was a male pointer—she went to work. She made calls to breeders, most of them in other parts of the country. Gen-erally, they tried to discourage her. Wrong dog, they'd say; get him an-other Brittany. She did find a couple of breeders who claimed their pointers were bred to work close, but they didn't have puppies of the right age. One had a nice female, and Marsha was about to make the deal, but Brooke insisted that the dog had to be a male so they kept looking. Then, through friends, she made contact with a woman who owned one of the big plantations in the area around Thomasville, Geor-gia—the Valhalla of quail hunting—and one of her dogs had a litter of pups just the right age. My wife made arrangements to have a dog shipped north as soon as it was weaned, which would be just in time for my birthday. Then, a couple of weeks later, the woman called to report that the pup had been killed by its mother.

Time was getting short, and my wife and daughters were getting desperate.

I was still in the dark, but then, I can be obtuse about this sort of thing. There were always conversations and lots of phone calls about things that didn't concern me, and I'd learned to ignore them. Several friends, however, knew about the great pointer search, and one of them told my wife and daughters about someone who lived in Bennington, Vermont, less than an hour away. They had pointers, and just might have a litter. They were reputed to be good hunting dogs.

My wife was skeptical, but she called the man, and yes, he did have a pointer bitch—and in fact, she'd recently whelped. They already had owners for most of the puppies, but there were a couple left. My wife and daughters drove down for a look that afternoon. When I asked where they were going, my wife said, "Shopping." Nobody asked if I wanted to go.

They didn't tell me that they were shopping for a puppy, which turned out to be even harder work than ordinary shopping. There aren't many hard and fast rules about buying a pup that you hope will, one day, become a good, working bird dog. There are a lot of theories, but most people just play hunches and go with the dubious advice of friends who claim to know. But when a pup is still nursing, you can't really tell if it will be any good or not. You won't know, for sure, until the dog is actually old enough to hunt whether it has a good nose or not, and whether it has the heart and brain to make it in the field.

But there is one rule that just about everyone agrees on—namely, that you should make sure of the breeding. If you don't know the bitch and the stud and what kind of dogs they are, then you should go with an established breeder. These can be found through several sources, including, these days, the Internet.

My wife didn't know anything about the people in Bennington, except that they had pointers, and that *maybe* they were good. She was flying blind. But time was short and she wanted a pointer. The man had given her the names of a couple of people she could call as references. They had bought pups from his earlier litters. She called and the people said, yes, they were satisfied with their dogs. She talked to one man who was a hunter and nearly rhapsodic about his dog. It was pretty thin, but it was all she had to go on.

The breeders turned out to be friendly, and they seemed to know, and love, pointers. The pups were just a little over five weeks old and still nursing when Marsha, Brooke, and Hadley saw them, squirming around and fighting for a nipple.

"They're so *cute*," Hadley said, and picked one up to cuddle. She was the animal person in the family. She had trained her own yellow Lab, Tickle, and had plans to breed her. My younger daughter was twelve, and spent her Saturdays at the animal shelter, taking care of abandoned and, for the most part, doomed pets. It was strictly volunteer work—no pay—and I had a hard time understanding why she wanted to spend her time that way. And, also, how she could bear it, knowing that most of the animals she cuddled were doomed to be euthanized.

"I love them," she said, simply. There wasn't much left to say after that.

"Which one do you want?" the owner asked.

"My dad wants a male," Brooke told him. "That's all I know."

"Well, there are two males left."

Take your pick, was the clear implication. But how to decide?

My wife and daughters did not know how to choose between two pups that still had not been weaned; but then, nobody really does. There didn't seem to be much difference, not even in their markings. They were both white with patches of liver, especially on their heads. They were both energetic and did a lot of squirming.

While there are theories about how to select a puppy from a litter, most experts seem to think you should just go on instinct. Someone once told me that it wasn't a bad idea to go with the runt of the litter, based on the idea that this was the pup that had to work the hardest to survive—the one that was always fighting for a nipple. If he made it, the runt would never grow up to be a timid dog, and you wanted your field dog to be assertive, at least, and maybe even aggressive.

But neither of the remaining males was the runt of this litter, so that theory was of no help to Marsha. One of the dogs did seem more interested in people than the other, who kept running away—to the extent that his short, unsteady legs would let him run at all. Hadley and Brooke wouldn't let him get very far, but whenever they put him down on the ground, he'd strike out for the territories—or the edge of the yard, anyway. By the time they left, he had exhausted himself and was sound asleep in a pile of puppies.

Marsha, Brooke, and Hadley agreed that the more social male pup was the one. Marsha paid the man, and said they would be back in a couple of weeks, when the dog had been weaned. The man said that would be fine. He'd have the papers and the veterinary records ready.

On the way home, there were some inevitable second thoughts. Maybe they'd made the wrong pick, Brooke said. Dad had said something about how he liked the way pointers ran and were tough; maybe they should have taken the bolder dog.

No, Hadley said, the dog wasn't *just* going to be a hunting dog. It was going to be a pet, too. And the dog they'd picked liked people. That was important.

Marsha agreed with that, and anyway, she said, the thing was done. The question now was, would Dad like his present?

The girls thought that was a sure thing. How could he not?

THREE

We went away for a couple of weeks, and when we came back, unbeknownst to me, Marsha called the man in Bennington to make arrangements for picking up the dog.

"I've got bad news," the man said, and told Marsha that the dog she had already paid for had died.

"Right about then, I started feeling like maybe this whole thing was cursed," she said to me, much later. "Maybe somebody was trying to tell me something." By this time, Jeb had been with us for a while, and he was a handful. "I probably should have listened," she said.

If the fates had a message, it probably was that a pointer was the wrong way to go. Or, that maybe it wasn't such a good idea to give someone a dog . . . any kind of dog. If you didn't like most presents, you could tell a lie, say it was just what you'd always wanted, and stick it in back of the closet or otherwise finesse it. But you couldn't very well do that with a dog. And you couldn't just take it back with the sales slip and exchange it, or get a refund. You were pretty much stuck with the dog, and that meant feeding it and taking it to the vet and giving it some kind of minimal training and affection, and then living with it for ten to fifteen years. And it meant a lot more than that, if you wanted the pup to be good in the field.

Still, Marsha is not easily deterred; not even when the fates are sending strong to urgent messages. She had settled on a male pointer pup as my birthday present, and that was how it was going to be. Only now, the pup she had paid for was dead, and my birthday was only a few days off. I don't imagine she concealed her disappointment from the breeder.

"The other male pup still hasn't been spoken for," the man told her, a little defensively. "He's available if you want. Otherwise, I'll certainly refund your money. And I'm very sorry."

"Let me think about it," she said.

That afternoon, she and the girls drove back to Bennington to look at the last pup in the litter. The one nobody seemed to want.

The pups had grown considerably since they'd last seen them. They were alert and steady on their legs, and showing a little independence. Especially the one that, if they agreed to the exchange, would belong to us.

Hadley picked one of his littermates up to cuddle while Marsha negotiated with the breeder. Hadley had the touch; the dog snuggled up to her and licked her face, and would have been content to stay in Hadley's little arms all day. She put that one down and picked up another and got the same response.

"Which one is ours?" she asked the man.

He pointed to the pup who was asleep on the ground, inside a small wire enclosure.

Hadley picked the pup up to cuddle it and the dog seemed fine. A bit of a squirmer, maybe, but not hostile or vicious or anything. Call it "active." Nothing wrong with an "active" dog; you don't want passivity, especially not in a field dog. But this pup was so restless that Hadley finally couldn't hold him any longer, and had to put him on the ground.

He immediately lit out for the territories.

"You'd better catch him," the breeder said. "There's no telling how far he might go."

So Hadley ran after the pup. His legs were still very short, and even when he was giving it all he had, he couldn't go very fast. She caught him, easily.

This would change.

Hadley brought the dog back to where he'd started, still trying to cuddle him, but he started squirming again and she put him down. Right away, he was on the move, heading for the tree line.

Hadley ran him down again. Now it was a game, and they played it for the time it took Marsha to agree to take this pup instead of the one she had paid for, and for the breeder to find and hand over the necessary papers—American Kennel Club registration and vet records. By then, Hadley was worn out and so was the pup.

"He really likes to run," Brooke said. "I guess pointers are like that." She didn't know the half of it.

The breeder agreed to keep the pup until the actual date of my birthday. Marsha had a big party planned for that night, out in our backyard with tables and lawn chairs, torchlights, champagne, and grilled beef tenderloin. She had invited thirty or forty of our friends, a couple of whom had come all the way from Alabama.

One of these was Winston Groom, known to the world as the author of *Forrest Gump*, which at this time was still merely a slightly obscure, if favorably reviewed, novel with a loyal following. The Tom Hanks film that was to become a national phenomenon had been shot and was due for release in less than a month. Winston had been through some difficult times with the movie people and didn't want to talk about it. This was all right, though, because there is always a lot to talk about with Winston. He is a big, insatiably gregarious man who thrives on company, people, and parties. Driving from Mobile, Alabama, to Dorset, Vermont, for a friend's birthday party had, typically, struck him as a capital idea, and I was touched by the gesture.

The party was going great—it was a fine, cool, late-summer evening in Vermont with lots of stars—and our guests were standing around in little groups, talking happily. There was music from a sound system and occasionally, someone would laugh very loudly and you would hear that sound over all the others. We'd eaten, and now someone brought out a cake with candles that I managed to blow out. Marsha had told our guests "no presents," but a couple of them had violated this edict and brought little gag gifts. Books on aging gracefully and the like. I'd made the usual protests and there had been the usual laughs. I toasted my friends and thanked them for coming. Then everyone went back to the party. Winston and I were catching up when my daughters appeared, holding a small box.

"Happy birthday," they said.

The box, I noticed, seemed to be moving. Whatever it held, I thought, it was plainly alive.

At this moment, I tumbled to what had been going on in plain sight for the last couple of months. All that talk about would I be getting another dog, and what kind of dog would it be, and what would I name it . . . there had been a point to all of it. I'd been dim to think otherwise, but there wasn't anything especially surprising about that.

"Say hello to your new dog," Hadley said, lifting the lid from the box and reaching in for the puppy.

She held him up for me and I got my first look at the dog that would, if things went right, be my companion for the next ten years or more.

You would need the professionally hard heart of W. C. Fields to resist any puppy. Fields famously stated, explicitly, that he didn't like children and *dogs*. Puppies get a pass, I believe, even from the most dedicated dog haters. They are the quintessential blend of innocence and exuberance, and when you look at a puppy you feel, somehow, younger. As part of her work with the animal shelter, Hadley had taken puppies on visits to the various old-age homes in the community.

"You know, Dad," she had told me after one of those visits, "it's amazing how much it cheers those people up. Playing with a puppy just makes them seem *happy*."

This was an empirical demonstration of something the great biologist E. O. Wilson had said to me, when I was interviewing him for a magazine article. He was trying to explain the concept of *Biophilia*, which, as I understand it, argues that there is a deep and natural sense of empathy among various creatures—that we all share some kind of wonder and delight at being alive, and we communicate it. "It is demonstrable fact," Wilson said, "that the companionship of an animal can improve the emotional and physical health of people who are old and alone and lack companionship."

These thoughts may, or may not, have flashed through my mind when I first laid eyes on my new puppy. Whatever thoughts I may have had, they were dwarfed by spontaneous and inchoate feelings of affection and delight. If all puppies are irresistible, then this one was even more so.

He was small, of course, but he had already passed through the round, blubbery, soft stage of growth. This pup had some definition. He was, as the bodybuilders would say, "cut." He had a full brisket and a narrow waist, and his ribs made a series of distinct ridges through his skin. He already had that lean and limber look of a hard-going pointer.

But it was the face, more than the body, that drew my attention and my feelings of complete affection. His head was angular, coming down from a high forehead to a long, almost aristocratic nose. His eyes were big, and he looked at me with an expression that was both alert and curious, and also, utterly fearless. I looked into his eyes and he looked right back into mine. I'd read, somewhere, that this was the test of an alpha dog. One that, if he'd stayed with his own kind instead of moving in with humans, would have been the leader of his pack. This pup was plainly no wimp.

"Oh, man," Winston said, "just what every man needs—a pointer pup. What are you going to do now, name him 'Bo' and move back to Alabama?"

"Nope," I said. "His name is Jeb Stuart, and he is going to strike fear into the hearts of Yankee birds all over this state."

◆

With the party going on around me, I tried holding Jeb, but he wasn't having any of it. He would squirm until I put him down, and then, he would take off toward the edge of the lawn where the light gave out on the border of a large meadow. It was all new country to him—and dark country, for that matter—but that didn't deter him. He wanted to get down on the ground and run.

"That dog," Winston said, "is going to run away from you from now until the end of time. I've seem 'em, and that's what they like to do."

"I'll bring him around," I said.

"Not happening, bro. That dog likes to run. Craves it."

Hadley finally found a leash and I clipped it to Jeb's little collar. I ran the loop of the leash around my wrist and put Jeb at my feet. I figured he'd run to the end of the leash, pull until he got the message, and then settle down.

Well, he ran out the slack in the leash, all right. Then, he kept on running; or tried to. He tugged until he was choking himself. Some of my guests turned with concerned looks when they heard him gasping for breath. The dog was strangling himself and was too determined—or something—to quit.

"He's okay," I said, picking Jeb up.

He promptly started struggling, so I put him back down and he ran instantly to the end of the leash and kept going. More sounds of distress from my pup as he fought for air and to break free from the leash and head for the hills.

"Come on, Jeb," I said, picking him up. "Give it a rest."

There was no reasoning with the pup. And you couldn't really get angry with him. He was too cute for that, and besides, there was something appealing about his determination. I figured there was no question that I had myself a "big-going dog."

But he was a distraction at my birthday party, and I finally turned him over to Hadley and asked her to keep an eye on him until the party was over. She agreed, and did her best. But Jeb still managed to break jail two or three times and make it out into the dark meadow. Then all the guests would walk out into the gloom calling for him and straining their eyes to catch a flash of white from a tiny pup. Someone would eventually find him and shout, "Here he is."

Once Jeb was safely on the leash or in someone's grasp, everyone would go back into the lighted section of my yard, find the drinks they had put down, and resume whatever conversations they had been having. Then, Jeb would make another escape and we would all put our drinks down and go on another puppy search.

"I'm telling you, Norman," Winston would say, "that dog is going to run away from you every chance he gets. He can't help himself. He's a pointer; it's his nature."

By the end of the party I'd stopped arguing.

It was, I remember thinking, interesting—at the very least—how one small dog could engage the full attention of thirty or forty adult humans just by running away. It seemed like an awful lot of leverage. Domination, almost.

It was a word I used many times over the next few years when people would tell me they were thinking about getting a dog and wondered if a pointer was the right breed for them. "Get used to the idea of having your life dominated by a dog," I'd say, "and you'll do fine."

FOUR

Jeb slept on the bedroom floor that night, on some old bedding I'd arranged for him. He didn't seem distressed by the strange surroundings or the separation from his mother and his littermates. I woke up when he did and put him outside and watched with a flashlight while he did his business. Then, when he looked like he was finished and was about to make a run for it, I would pick him up and bring him back inside and put him down on his bed where he would curl up and go back to sleep. I would watch him for a while, feeling a kind of mysterious delight that recalled the way I would watch my baby daughters, asleep in their cribs, in the first days after we'd brought them home. It was a restless night for me. Jeb did fine.

In the morning, I fed Jeb and took him for a walk around the yard. While I watched, he would study the ground and decide on the place that he wanted to be, then run to it, full speed. When he got there, he would stop, sniff around a little and study things, then pick another place and run to it as fast as his short legs would carry him. It looked random, but I thought there had to be some kind of logic to it. He knew where he wanted to go and he went there in a hurry. If this was play—and, superficially, it looked like it was—then there was a point to it.

As I watched him at work, something suddenly registered on my brain; something I'd noticed the night before but hadn't really thought about. It was the dog's tail. Jeb did not have the long, straight tail that is typical of pointers. His was curled around in an arc so that the point almost touched his back between his hips. His tail looked like a sickle.

I'd never seen a pointer with a sickle tail before, and as I watched the pup, I decided that I kind of liked the look. There was something both idiosyncratic and jaunty about it. But he wouldn't, I realized, have the classic pointer look when he was pointing birds—the front foot raised, the head thrust forward in the direction of the scent he was making, and the tail high, straight, and erect . . . pointing in the opposite direction. It was, I decided, a minor flaw, and one that I could easily live with.

A few days later, however, while doing some superficial research, I learned that most serious pointer breeders consider a sickle tail a fatal flaw and would cull any pup who had one. They might try to give the dog away, but most of the time, they would not find a taker and the dog would be put down. So Jeb's tail, then, was normally a fatal deformity. He'd escaped execution only because the breeder was an amateur who liked pointers and bred them for pets as well as for sporting dogs, and was too soft-hearted to put a dog down just because his tail had a curl to it.

This accounted—in part, anyway—for why my dog was the last one in the litter to find a home. It didn't have anything to do with character; it was all about a cosmetic defect. When I learned this, it made me feel even more attached to Jeb. I felt a kind of defensiveness and protectiveness toward him. The tail wasn't his fault; in fact, he certainly wasn't aware that there was anything wrong with the way he looked. I imagined that in his mind, however mysteriously it worked, he was a normal pointer dog and proud of it. And in the inevitable way dog owners have of anthropomorphizing their pets, I saw him as a dog who had been given an unfair shake by the dark forces of biology but would, through grit and character, prevail.

In short, I came to love him all the more fiercely for his flaw.

After our tour of the yard, I took Jeb to the office with me. I'd been renting a room in the upstairs of a building that belonged to one of the local real estate firms. It was easier than working at home while my daughters were still in school. Even when the housing market was booming, the real estate office was quieter than my house.

Two of the agents were at their desks when I arrived with Jeb, and as soon as we walked in, they were all over the pup, petting him and cooing at him. Jeb took it like a man.

"What kind of dog is he?" an agent named Kathy asked.

"He's a pointer," I said. "Actually, if you want to be proper about it, he's an English pointer."

"A hunting dog," she said, "like the ones you see on calendars?"

"That's right."

"What about his tail, though," her colleague, Laura, said. "Is it supposed to be crooked like that?"

"Well, no. Not typically."

"Will it straighten out?"

"I don't know. But I don't think so."

"Well, I think it's cute."

"Yes," I said. "So do I. But I'd prefer 'distinguished.'"

She liked that.

"That's right," she said, rubbing Jeb's ears and his tummy. "You have a very distinguished tail. Such a handsome little man."

I took Jeb up to the office and closed the door. I made a bed for him and put out a small bowl of water and a little rawhide strip for him to chew on. He went right to work on it while I settled in behind the desk.

I didn't get much work done that first morning. Jeb was too curious about the things in the office. There were extension cords that he could chew on, and a little closet that he could get into through a door that wouldn't close completely. And when he got bored with that, he would whimper for some action so I would stop what I was doing and play with him. He was a distraction, but I was happy for it.

I could have left the dog at home with my daughters who hadn't started back to school yet and would have been delighted to watch him and play with him. They'd been disappointed, in fact, when I said I would be taking him to work with me.

But I had a plan.

I'd done the obedience training myself with my first bird dog—Molly, the Brittany—working on a theory I'd gotten from books and from other dog owners. The idea was that you "bonded" with your dog from the earliest possible age. You wanted the dog to think of you not as some remote force issuing commands, but as a companion and partner. This way, the dog learned to like being in your company and to do what you wanted done, not from fear of punishment, but from a desire to please you. This, he came to realize, was the way to make life pleasant.

The idea of bonding with a dog seemed more humane and agreeable on the face of it than the old methods of "force training," which involved a lot of heavy punishment and harsh commands. And, according to its advocates, bonding paid off when you took the dog into the field. A dog that was accustomed to being with you more or less constantly was less likely to run off and hunt on his own, or otherwise freelance. This was the theory, anyway.

But it was a long, long way from the methods people had used on the pointers I'd known when I was a kid.

◆

I was probably twelve when I first went out bird hunting with a man who owned pointers. A friend of the family, he was a man who liked hunting and enjoyed taking kids out. I knew him as a patient, gentle person, so I was surprised when he let his two dogs out of the truck and, almost immediately, began talking to them in tones that sounded, to my young ears, harsh at best. He wasn't yelling, but there was something beyond mere firmness in the way he talked to those dogs.

The dogs had been riding in the back of the truck on the way out to the little patch farm where we started out, and when he dropped the tailgate, he didn't take time to pat either of the dogs or say anything affectionate or kind. It was merely, "All right, Belle, let's get with it now. You, too, Bo. Get out there and find some birds."

The dogs milled around for a second or two, first taking care of their bladders and then checking the tires for scent. One of them approached me and I held out a hand to pat the dog.

"Hey," the man said sharply, "I said get on and hunt some birds."

The dogs turned away and headed out for a fence line that was grown up thick with brush. When they hit a patch of briars, they hesitated, looking for a way in.

"Don't be playing that game with me. Get on in there."

The dogs dove into the briars.

It seemed a little cold, but I was new to this and a kid, so I didn't say anything; I merely loaded my gun and followed the man's lead. His eyes were on the dogs, and he watched them like a prison guard supervising a reluctant road gang, alert for the first sign of malingering.

"Hunt 'em up, now. Don't be cruising the country. Hunt birds."

It sounded something like the way farmers talked to a difficult mule. The commands weren't meant to be specific. The point was to establish who was in charge and to make sure no one forgot it.

I was soft and innocent, I suppose, and a little disillusioned. I'd thought that the relationship between man and hunting dog would be . . . oh, I don't know, maybe friendly and collegial. You were supposed to be in this thing together, after all. The dog was doing you a service, finding birds for you and then pointing them. There ought to be more camaraderie. Or something.

But I got over these qualms as soon as the dogs found the first covey. I was watching one of them lope through the broomweed, when it suddenly stopped almost in mid-stride. What had been all fluid movement at one moment was, in an instant, absolute stillness. A stillness so complete the dog could have been turned to stone. Then, when the other dog saw that the first one had stopped, she did the same thing. Both dogs were now fixed firmly to the ground. It was a stunning, beautiful sight, and I stopped, too, so that I could admire it.

The man I was hunting with didn't have time, however, to appreciate the poetry of the scene.

"Got a point. Keep moving," he merely said, "let's walk in on 'em. Keep your eyes ahead, where the birds will be coming up."

I tried to do what I'd been told, but my eyes kept going back to those two dogs, standing staunch on point. I'd never seen anything like it.

"Come on, now," the man said to me, almost in the same tone he used with the dogs. And I hurried to keep up.

When we walked past the first dog, I could see that while he was standing steady, the muscles under the skin were quivering with anticipation. I felt my own body singing with the same kind of eagerness.

The birds came up in a blur and a startling explosion of whirring wings. I'm sure that I almost dropped the gun at the sound and sight of perhaps twenty little brown shapes angling off, it seemed, in every direction in front of me. I threw the gun to my shoulder and tried to shoot into the melee, but forgot to take the safety off. By the time I got off a shot, it was in hopeless desperation. The birds were out of range but it didn't make any difference; I wasn't aiming at anything, anyway.

When things were quiet again, the dogs were still standing on point. Through it all, they hadn't moved.

The man said, "You get one?"

"No, sir," I said. Meekly.

"Covey rises are hard at first," he said kindly. "You'll get better but you don't ever get to where it doesn't surprise you. I've been doing this for thirty years and I still get shook."

"Did you get one?" I said.

"Two," he said, and put his whistle in his mouth.

He blew a sharp note and said, "Okay, dead birds. Come on, hunt 'em up. Hunt dead."

At the sound of the whistle, the dogs were off point and moving, working the grass. It was like that game you played in school, where you point to someone and say, "Freeze." Your victim is supposed to hold his exact posture until you say, "Unfreeze." Then, he can move again.

At the first note of that whistle, the dogs were in motion again, noses to the ground, looking for the birds the man had shot.

"Hunt 'em up," he said, firmly. "Hunt dead."

One of the dogs moved off a little from where the birds had gone down, and the man shouted, "Get in here, Belle. Dammit! Hunt dead."

The dog turned instantly and did what she was told.

Each dog found a bird. They picked them up with their mouths and brought them in to the man's outstretched hand. When he took a bird, he looked at it for a moment, then said, "Okay. Find another, now. Hunt birds."

No praise. No pats. Just a brusque "Hunt birds."

We hunted on until noon and found some more birds. My shooting, however, had not improved by the time we quit for lunch. I'd shot, several times, but still hadn't cut a feather, and I was discouraged.

The man loaded his dogs in the bed of the truck and we drove to one of those old country stores that you once saw everywhere in Alabama. A sagging, weathered old building that, if it had ever been painted, showed no sign that it had been done recently, or that it would do any good to try it again. There were some metal soft-drink and chewing-tobacco signs nailed to the outside walls, and they were so old that the colors had faded in the sunlight to almost a single hue. There were patches of rust along the edges of the signs and around the holes where they had been nailed to the walls. There was a porch on the building and a dog was lying there, sleeping in the shade. A single gas pump stood sentry in front of the store. You could imagine that the usual sale was for "a dollar's worth."

That kind of place.

The man left the dogs in the bed of the truck—on leashes so they couldn't escape and pick a fight with the hound sleeping on the porch—and we went inside and bought sardines, tuna fish, saltines, and soft drinks.

"A South Alabama seafood platter," the man I was hunting with called it.

"You finding any birds?" the owner of the store asked when he took the man's money.

"We got into a few coveys," he said. "Had us a good morning."

We ate on the porch and he talked to me about quail hunting.

"You ain't doing so bad," he said. "A lot of people never even get the gun to their shoulder the first time a covey of quail gets up in front of them. They just freeze. But you got the gun mounted and you got off some shots."

"I didn't hit anything, though."

"No," he said. "I'd say you do need to work on that part of it."

"How?"

"Well, I suspect you are probably doing what most people do when they start out."

"What's that?"

"Flock shooting. You see all those birds in the air in front of you and you figure that if you just throw some lead in there amongst them, you're bound to hit something."

I nodded. He had that right.

"It ain't that easy. But, then, it isn't as hard as you're thinking it is right now, either. What you need to remember—and keep telling yourself, over and over, because you aren't going to believe it—is that those birds aren't as quick as they look. They aren't flying fast enough to break the sound barrier. Most of the time on a covey rise, you've got enough time to mount your gun and pick out a single bird—the one on your outside shoulder is generally best—and track him. *Just* him, now; shut all those other birds out of mind and just concentrate on him, move with him, and pull the trigger. He'll fall, and when he does, find you another and do the same thing with him. But that's for later . . . shooting doubles. Right now, just concentrate on the one bird."

"All right," I said. It sounded like good advice, and, anyway, I couldn't do any worse.

"We didn't go after any of the singles this morning," he said, "because they all flew down into that gum swamp. Shooting singles is easier than shooting them on the covey rise. You can concentrate since you don't have all those other birds in the air to distract you. Maybe we'll get a chance or two on some singles the next couple of places we hunt. Get you some action anyway."

I nodded.

"But other than the fact that you didn't put any birds on the ground," he said, "how did you like your first day of quail hunting?"

"It was great," I said with conviction, because I meant it. I'd read a lot of stories about quail hunting and been primed to do it. And, except for my shooting, it had been that rare thing that measures up. None of that vague sense of disappointment you experience when something doesn't quite deliver the way you had dreamed it would—and that, in most cases, it never could have.

No. I was already passionate about quail hunting and the reason was simple: It came down to the dogs. All morning, I'd had a hard time taking my eyes off of them. Even when I needed to look down to cross a ditch or a fence, my eyes would be drawn irresistibly back up to look at the dogs. I didn't want to miss that moment when one of them made game and locked down on point. Just watching them course the broomweed—methodical, intense, and all business—was ceaselessly fascinating, and it stirred something in me. The dogs had the dignity that comes with purpose and with being serious about your work.

"It's even better than I thought it would be," I added. "Except for my shooting."

"And that will improve," he said. "Got to, doesn't it. Can't get any worse."

I smiled and said, "No sir. That's for sure." I didn't mind the teasing. Welcomed it, actually. It made me feel like an equal.

"Well," the man said, "I'm like you, that way. Quail hunting is one of the few things in this life I just can't get enough of. If it was whiskey, I'd be a drunk for sure. I tried deer hunting, a little, and never cared for it. Same with ducks. I'll go if someone invites me, but I'm not rushing out to buy me a boat and a layout of decoys, then start in building blinds down in the delta. But quail hunting . . . There's only two weekends I've missed bird hunting during the season in the last five years— once to go to a funeral, and the other time when a friend invited me to the Alabama/Auburn game. It was a good game and Alabama won, but I was miserable the whole time. I wanted to be bird hunting.

"I like the walking and the way you hunt with a partner, for starters. When you hunt deer, you're down in the hardwoods in the river bottoms by yourself, and I'm just not that good a company. I'd rather have someone to talk to.

"And, of course, you have to like these little birds. I read something, once, that said the bobwhite is a gentleman, and I think that's right. He's got beautiful colors without being gaudy, and he holds tight and doesn't just take off and flush wild. He flies hard and he is surely good to eat.

"But the thing I like most about quail hunting is the dog work. That's something special. I could imagine myself coming out and not even shooting; just watching the dogs. They're the real stars of this show."

"Yes, sir," I said. I knew exactly what he meant and already had the same feeling, in a primitive, youthful way. He'd shot a lot of birds and

I'd only shot into the air where the birds were flying in a confusing blur. I was miles and years from reaching his stage of wisdom, but I could see clearly how it was possible, and I wanted to get there.

Which made the way he seemed to feel about his dogs all the more confusing to me. If he appreciated their work so strongly, why didn't he seem to feel more affection—even love—for his dogs?

I didn't ask. Wasn't sure how to phrase the question without sounding impertinent, and, besides, we were finished eating and it was time to get back to hunting.

"I even like the lunches," he said. "How about you? You enjoy your seafood platter?"

"It was great."

"You don't have to sugarcoat it for me, son," he said. "It's enough you like the bird hunting."

We hunted all afternoon, until the light began to fade, the air turned cool, and the blackbirds—we called them "ricebirds"—began to fly over in flocks of a hundred or more. I never did hit a bird on the covey rise, but I did get a couple of singles.

On the first, one of the dogs was locked down in a point so tight and firm that you thought, inevitably, of something coiled. A spring or even a snake. Every muscle and fiber of the dog's body was taut and straining, and as I walked in on him, it seemed almost impossible that he could hold the stance. It was that rigid and unnatural. He was like one of those sentries I'd seen at the Tomb of the Unknown Soldier on a school trip to Washington, D.C.

There was duty and discipline in the dog's intense immobility, and I felt a kind of awe about it.

The bird flushed at my feet and angled off to the left, which was the side where I shot, if not well, then at least better. I got the gun up and tracked the bird and was not even aware of touching the trigger. I saw him go down in a puff of feathers.

"Good *shot*," the man said, and he sounded even happier than I felt. He blew on his whistle and commanded the dog to "Hunt dead."

The dog broke from his point like a football player hearing the snap count and went to the spot. He picked the bird up and brought it to the man's hand. He took the bird and tossed it to me. It was a cock, with the distinctive white feathers on its head, and it felt small, dry, and limp in my palm. Still warm, with a drop or two of blood showing but otherwise undamaged. The dog had a soft mouth; one more thing for me to marvel over.

I admired the bird for a moment or two. I'd been on dove fields and had shot my share—for a kid, anyway—but the feeling was nothing like this. Those had been randomly passing birds and you took shots as they came to you. There was something a little . . . oh, *passive* about it. Maybe that was why you talked about a "dove *shoot*" as opposed to a "quail *hunt*." Though I don't suppose I was doing that kind of linguistic analysis at that moment. I was too young and too full of feelings of triumph and pride and a sense, as well, of being teammates with the dog. It was *our* bird. We were partners in the glory.

I wanted to reward the dog somehow. Pat him, maybe, or at least give him a few words of praise. But he didn't have time for that, and neither did the man I was hunting with. They were back at work before I slipped the limp body of the bird into the game pouch of my vest.

The bird weighed only a few ounces, but I was aware of its tiny bulk over my hip and it felt good there. I was a quail hunter, now. Blooded, and all of that. And while I can't remember thinking it, I must have been imagining how it would be when I would be hunting, some day, with dogs of my own.

At the end of the day, I felt the pleasant, leg-weary sense of fatigue that you don't mind when you are a kid because you expect it to pass quickly. We rode back to the man's house and when we got there, he unloaded the dogs, and instead of bringing them into the house, took them to the kennel out in the backyard. He brushed the burrs out of their coats and gave them each a bowl of what looked to me like very meager rations. A cup or so of dried dog food with a little bacon grease poured over the top.

"The fat," he explained, "is good for their coats."

He did tell them they'd done "good work," but not with a lot of conviction. Then he closed the kennel door and when we left them, the dogs were devouring their suppers. It all seemed very impersonal.

I had expected, I suppose, that he would have taken them inside with him when he got home and that the dogs would have curled up at his feet, in front of the fire, while he cleaned his shotgun and had something adult to drink. Instead, the dogs stayed in the kennel while we plucked the birds in the kitchen. The dogs had done their part of the job and that was that. They would stay in the kennel until it was time for them to come out and go to work again.

"Do they ever come inside?" I asked the man.

"No, son. Those aren't house dogs," he said. "They're *working* dogs."

He said it like it was an obvious distinction and no more needed to be said.

"Oh," I said. Like I understood entirely.

I didn't, but that didn't diminish the glow that I felt at the end of the day. It stayed with me until I got under the covers that night and fell asleep with the image of those two determined, hardworking dogs doing their jobs out in front of me, weaving through the broomweed, looking for scent, and then locking up in a posture of pure purpose when they found it. It was a picture as indelible as it was thrilling, and I couldn't wait until I could see it again. And again.

FIVE

My program, in the early days with my new dog, was to build a relationship unlike the one the man who'd introduced me to bird hunting had with his pointers. It was not going to be strictly business with Jeb and me. For starters, he was going to live in the house, and he needed to learn to act like a gentleman, especially around the ladies—my wife and my two daughters. Jeb, I decided, needed to learn how to be with people. If necessary, he needed to learn how to *like* being around people. Turned out, this was something I didn't have to worry about. There was no need to "socialize" Jeb. He liked hanging with people.

But, I didn't know this at the time, so I took him to the office every day and he rode in the passenger seat of my truck when I ran errands. He slept on a little mat at the foot of the bed and he was generally treated like my sidekick and a member of the family.

Puppies always get a pass, of course, and can get away with things that no fully grown dog could. They can chew your shoes and tear up the carpet and pee on the sofa, but because they are cute, they generally get away with it. You might scold them a little, but they merely have to look hurt or frightened for you to relent and feel guilty for brutalizing such an innocent little creature. Inevitably, you try to make up with the dog and, so, he wins.

Actually, in the first few weeks he was with us, Jeb behaved pretty decently. He was very easy to housebreak. This took only a day or two before he knew to go to the door and stamp his little feet to let me know he wanted to go out. When he "made a mistake," I would pick him up and take him out so he would get the message, and this quickly did the trick.

"He's a real smart dog," I said to my wife, already indulging in the bragging that makes so many dog owners insufferable.

Nobody in the house seemed to mind, though. My wife and daughters were as smitten with Jeb as I was. He had, in the age-old way of dogs, ingratiated himself with the people who fed and sheltered him, and had bent them pretty much to his will. Jeb had become the focus of the household and none of us minded one little bit. If we were all in a room somewhere, and he wasn't there, we would go find him. But usually, he was right with us.

Jeb was plainly a "people dog." If you were sitting in a chair or on the sofa, he would come up to your feet and raise himself so he was on his haunches, with both front paws in the air, and ask to be petted or picked up. He got his wish and spent a lot of time in laps, getting his ears rubbed and his flanks stroked, which he seemed to like a lot.

"A lap dog is not really what I had in mind," I said to Marsha one day. "Especially not from a pointer."

"Well, it looks like you're going to have to get used to it," she said.

I didn't mind, really, though this was a long way from what my childhood experience with pointers had led me to expect. I was no longer worrying about whether Jeb would adapt to people and learn to be a congenial house dog. Now, I sometimes wondered if this excessive domestication would make him less enthusiastic when it came time to go out into the field and do what he had been bred to do.

Turned out, I had no reason for concern. As Jeb got older, he got right with the program when I did things to sharpen his instincts and his interest in hunting birds. I had an old grouse wing, saved from the previous bird season, and I tied it with a piece of string to the end of a fly rod. I would dangle the bird wing on the ground in front of Jeb, about ten feet from his nose, and when he rushed it, I would jerk the wing into the air, out of his reach.

Then, we would do it again. After a few misses, Jeb would begin to creep in on the wing, instead of rushing it, and when he got close and stopped, I would tell him he was a good boy and reach down to pat him. He gradually learned to sneak like that and then pause and wait for the compliment and the strokes. I'd picked this method up from one of the many books on dog training that I'd bought and studied. According to them, this was the way to teach a young dog how to point birds. I was delighted at how well it worked.

After he'd gotten pretty good on the wing, I started working with him on the most difficult—and important—command that any dog learns. According to the experts I was reading and talking to, if you can make a bird dog respond to the command "Whoa," you have pretty much won the battle. If your dog is making game but getting too close and flushing birds before you are in range, you merely tell him to "Whoa." The dog stops until you are in range and then you release him and let him move in closer until—you devoutly hope—he stops on point. You then move in for the flush and life is good.

"Whoa" also enables you to stop a dog that is running wild or has gotten too far out ahead of you or is about to cross a road heedlessly and get run over by some guy who has his foot all the way down to the pickup's floor. In short, once you have "Whoa" down, you are in control. "Whoa" allows you to stop everything and get your dog gathered up. You almost wish there were someone who could do the same for you, now and then.

So Hadley and I went to work on "Whoa." We would take Jeb out into the yard. Hadley would hold Jeb on a leash and stand on one side of the yard while I took a position thirty or forty feet away. When I called to Jeb, Hadley would release him, and as he was coming to me, I would throw up both hands and shout, "Whoa!"

At first, Jeb reacted in utter confusion. Sometimes, he would run back to Hadley. Sometimes, he would come to me. Now and then, he would head for the safety of the house. But we stayed with it, day after day, working for ten or fifteen minutes at a time. Longer than that and the dog would lose interest and the whole exercise became pointless.

After several days of this, I was beginning to wonder if Jeb might have some kind of congenital resistance to learning this command. Hadley, however, saw through the problem. She was, as usual, much more intuitive than I.

She had a touch with dogs and had trained her own Labrador, Tickle, to retrieve to hand signals. She'd done this on her own, using a plastic dummy that she would throw into the yard, telling Tickle to "fetch." She worked tirelessly with the dog, never raising her voice or showing any sign whatsoever of impatience. When the dog made a mistake or simply looked confused, she would pick up the dummy, return with the dog to their starting position, and do it all again. Tickle adored her; every afternoon during the school year, precisely at 3:00 P.M., she would scratch at the door to be let out and then walk down our driveway to wait for the school bus. When she saw the big yellow shape, she would starting pacing and wagging her tail, and when Hadley came down the steps, Tickle would rush her and wait for her hugs.

So Hadley had the touch, and in a month or so of work, had Tickle trained up about as far as an amateur can possibly get with a retrieving dog. It had been touching to watch. The only setback in the whole program had not been Hadley's fault. Or Tickle's, for that matter. For some mysterious genetic reason, Tickle could not stand the scent or taste of ducks. One morning when I came home with a mallard I'd shot on the Battenkill River, Hadley and I took Tickle out in the yard and threw the duck out on the grass for her to retrieve. Tickle stayed obediently at Hadley's side until she was released with the command to "fetch." She then ran straight to the duck and picked it up with her mouth, just like she did with the training dummy.

Then, without taking a single step, she spat the duck out and backed off, giving it a look that said, unmistakably, that she thought it was vile and that wild horses could not get her to put that nasty thing in her mouth again.

Still, Hadley plainly knew what she was doing when it came to working with dogs. So when we were about to start another session with Jeb, working on "Whoa," and she said, "Dad, will you let me try something?"—I listened.

"Sure, kid. What do you have in mind?"

"Why don't *you* hold him on the leash and let me call him?"

"Okay," I said. I couldn't see how it would make any difference, one way or the other.

Hadley took her place, and when she called to Jeb, I let him off the leash. He ran to her and when he was halfway there, Hadley held out her hand like a cop stopping traffic and said, gently, "Whoa, Jeb."

He stopped for a second and Hadley said, "Good boy, Jeb."

He liked that, and ran to her to be rewarded with strokes and more kind words. When he got to her, Hadley picked him up and took him back to the spot where he'd stopped. She held him there and said, "Whoa, Jeb. Good boy. Whoa, Jeb." Then she released him and backed away. He stayed on the spot this time, looking a little confused but holding his ground as long as those "Good boy" words were coming his way.

We repeated the drill until he lost interest. Then we did it again the next day and the next. In a week or so, Jeb was stopping whenever Hadley said, "Whoa." And eventually, he would do it for me, too.

Those were good times, Hadley and Jeb and me working on the lawn. I'm sure I would never have made any progress with Jeb, working alone. I was too impatient and too determined to achieve some kind of impossible perfection. Hadley, on the other hand, had a feel for the thing and a tolerance for the fact that Jeb was merely a puppy. What I'd sometimes judged—far too harshly, I'm ashamed to say—as a passive personality in my daughter, was something else. It was a gentleness of spirit that many people, even kids, would have tried to conceal or compensate for in an age that celebrates toughness and aggression. Hadley wouldn't give in to this impulse, which I came to appreciate and admire much later—when times got tough—as a greater kind of strength.

At the end of our training sessions, I would sometimes feel like I had learned as much from Hadley as Jeb had.

"Isn't this neat," Hadley said to me, one day, when we had finished up and were watching Jeb romping aimlessly on the lawn. "It's just so much fun."

"It surely is," I said.

As promising as those first sessions were, I was still a little concerned that I might be nurturing the wimp side of my dog's personality. This was doubtless caused mostly by my previous experiences with pointers and the conventional wisdom that I had, over the years, assimilated about the breed.

Pointers were famously hardheaded dogs. "You got to lay up the side of a pointer's head with a two-by-four just to get his attention," was the sort of line you heard when I was growing up and learning to hunt birds. Back then, I never saw a single pointer that was treated remotely like a pet, and some hunters of my experience were borderline brutal to their dogs. A couple even crossed the line.

I remember hunting with a man who had a pointer that he paid someone else to keep for him. He didn't want the hassle of feeding the dog and worrying about keeping track of him, so he left him with a farmer who put him out back in a shed. Between bird seasons, the only human contact the dog ever had came twice a day when the farmer would feed him and let him out to stretch his legs and do his business before locking him up again. During the season, the owner would come by to pick the dog up and take him out to hunt. The dog would ride in the trunk of the man's car.

The dog's name was Gus, and he was, in fact, plenty hardheaded and impulsive. The first time we took him out, he found a dead pig and rolled in it until his coat was covered with a kind of gooey, gray slime. He stunk to the heavens, but somehow still pointed birds.

I learned, much later, that this business of rolling in some particularly fragrant mess is a deeply genetic impulse that can be traced back to dogs' most celebrated ancestors—namely wolves. One theory is that wolves would roll in something dead and then return to the pack wearing the fragrance like a flashy new set of threads. The stink was a trophy, then, and added to the wearer's social status. Modern researchers consider this a stretch, since today's dogs demonstrably do *not* get a status bump when they return to *their* pack—suburban owners, for instance—smelling like a maggoty woodchuck carcass. Quite the opposite. This evolutionary *raison* for rolling in something foul and dead doesn't seem to hold up.

Another theory for this kind of repellent behavior is that the wolves were using the aroma of something dead to mask their own scent, thus enabling them to sneak up on prey. This theory seems more plausible than the one that equates stink with social status. But a more compelling hypothesis is that while dogs are interested in acquiring the smell of the dead thing for themselves, they are more interested in leaving *their* scent on the carcass. Just as they mark territory by urine, they let other dogs—or wolves—who are drawn to the smell of the dead thing know that they are in the area.

The impulse, then, is not some sort of random weirdness from which a dog can be "broken," but deeply hardwired into the genes. Something dog owners—especially if the dog is one of the hunting breeds and spends a lot of time in the field—just have to get used to. This was certainly true, as I learned later, of my pointer. Eventually, I simply stopped trying to persuade Jeb that smelling like a garbage truck was not the way to win friends or, even, be allowed inside at night, and I started investigating the best deodorizing methods.

But that was later, long after that first experience with dogs and nasty-smelling dead animals, when old Gus found himself a fine, dead pig to roll in.

Gus's owner and I tried to stay downwind from him for the rest of the day, but this wasn't always possible, and the smell was rank enough to turn my stomach.

"That stupid, hardheaded sonofabitch," my partner grumbled. "My car is going to smell for a week."

Gus had other ways of irritating his owner, or, perhaps, of paying him back for dumping him with an indifferent keeper and then coming around only when he needed someone to do a day job of finding a few quail. For one thing, he was exceedingly good at running away.

Some days, his owner told me, Gus would just take off and never come back. The man would call and call, fire his gun into the air, go back to the car and blow the horn—and none of it would work. Gus would be off on walkabout, and eventually the man would get in his car and go on home. The dog had a collar and sooner or later, some farmer or logger would call and say he'd found Gus, and did the man want to come and pick him up.

"I'd feel like saying, 'No. You keep him or shoot him or turn him loose again. I don't care.' But I'd always go out and get him. Sometimes he'd be all cut up, like he'd been in a fight, or stinking from something he'd been rolling in. But he'd just look at me like, 'Where have you been?', and then he'd get in the trunk and I'd take him back to where he was living, and he'd get out and go to the shed with his head hanging down like a convict who'd escaped and been caught and now he was going to be doing solitary on bread and water for thirty days. But the hardheaded fool never learns."

Gus didn't exactly run *away* that first time I hunted with him. But he did range. We'd see him way out, maybe a half mile away, charging through the brush and the briars. The man would holler at him to come in and "hunt close," but the futility of this was almost laughable. If Gus actually heard him, it didn't register enough in his brain for him to even turn his head. He was on a mission.

"He *will* cover some ground," his owner said, in forlorn tones. "I'll give him that. No one will ever accuse old Gus of being underfoot."

On a couple of occasions, when Gus was just a white blur on the horizon, we would see him stop and go on point.

"Let's go," my partner would say, and we would unload the guns, hold them at a kind of port-arms position, and take off. It was hard work, running in boots over ground that was pocked with the occasional gopher hole or root extrusion. We tripped and went down face-first more than once. But we couldn't take the time to walk up on the dog. He would hold a point . . . but not that long. We were on the clock.

When we got close enough, say twenty yards, we'd stop, panting and sweating, and reload. Then we would try to walk in on the dog. My eyes would be blurred with sweat and my chest would be heaving, but for the first few steps it seemed worth it. There was Gus up ahead, and for all his flaws and failings, the dog had a *stylish* point, head low to the ground, tail high, one front leg raised and cocked. The look was just so perfect that you were willing to grant the dog an indulgence.

Then, while we were still out of range, he would drop that front paw and take a step.

"No, Gus, no. Whoa. *Whoa!*"

The shouting worked in a fashion exactly contrary to the wishes of Gus's owner. When the shouting started, Gus would stop creeping and rush the covey, which would flush, out of range, and scatter. If the birds flew into a gum swamp where we couldn't follow them, then Gus would simply start rambling again, as though nothing had happened.

Birds? What birds? I didn't see any birds!

If, on the other hand, the birds fanned out in the grass where we could hunt up the singles, then Gus would take off after them and start putting them up, one by one, until they were all dispersed and it was hopeless to try to mark them.

49

Then he would resume his ramble as though nothing had happened.

His owner would swear, up and down, that he was going to take that worthless, no-account, sorry-assed sonofabitch to the pound, first thing Monday morning, and they could do their worst with him.

Gus ran a couple of rabbits that first day and one deer. He would take off after them, running like he was on fire, with the owner screaming for him to "Whoa." But he might as well have been commanding Gus to sit up and sing "Anchors Aweigh." Hard as the dog was running, I was surprised that he didn't catch the rabbits, anyway, and who knows, maybe even that deer.

But after a while, we'd see old Gus, back on the hunt, five hundred yards up ahead and still cruising. The dog had stamina.

And, for all our frustrations, old Gus did deliver a couple of times that day. Just enough, I think, to keep him from being delivered to the pound when it opened for business on Monday morning.

Just before lunch, Gus was running a ridge of big, old longleaf pine with wire grass growing under the trees. He was out pretty far, but we could see him—and this was a point in his favor and about as good as things had been that day. Gus was moving from side to side, at a lope, and suddenly he stopped like he had run into a glass wall.

"Is he—" I started to say.

"He damn sure is. Let's go."

So we did the drill with unloading the guns and double-timing up to where old Gus was standing, striking his elegant point like he was a field-trial champ, going for the trophy.

We reloaded and started walking in.

"Steady, Gus. *Steady.*" The man implored.

I silently begged the same of Gus, expecting the worst. But he held his ground, and we were soon close enough to smell him and then to see his lips quivering and his nose twitching.

Then we were by him and he was still steady, and just as I had decided that it was a false point, or that Gus was on something other than birds—a gopher tortoise, maybe, or a possum—the covey got up.

The flush was explosive, as always, but maybe because I had given up on it, the sound and the blur didn't rattle me as much as usual. I got the gun up and tracked the outside bird and brought him down in a conclusive little puff of feathers. I believe I must have whooped when the bird fell.

I tried to find another but was too eager and shot too soon. It would be a long time before I dropped my first double.

Still, I had shot a bird on the covey rise. And so, it turned out, had my partner.

I stood fixed to the ground, still under the spell of the flush and my triumph, expecting the retrieve. But my partner broke the mood.

"Go get your bird," he said urgently. "*Quick!*"

He plainly wasn't fooling. There were still a few feathers in the air, marking the area where the bird had fallen, so I hustled over to the spot and picked up the bird, which was in plain sight in the grass.

My partner did the same with his bird.

"Gus will sometimes retrieve them," he said, a little apologetically, "and sometimes not. And every now and then, he'll retrieve them and *eat* them. Hard as we worked for these birds, we don't need that."

Gus, meanwhile, had other things in mind. The singles had fanned out across the low, back side of the ridge, and he was eager to hunt them, almost as though he'd had a conversion experience, had seen—at long last—the light, and now knew what his proper calling in life was. He was a bird dog, by God, and he was going to do it right.

And he did. He pointed four or five singles and we shot them and made the retrieves ourselves. For twenty or thirty minutes, we had bird hunting with Gus as it was meant to be. All was right and, except for the rancid, greasy smell of that dead pig wafting on the December breeze, the tableau was perfect.

There were still several birds scattered through the broomweed, and Gus wanted to hunt them, when my partner said, "We've hit this covey pretty hard. Let's leave the rest for seed and go find us another."

This didn't seem like a bad idea—especially now that Gus was hearing the music. We finally got him to leave the ridge and hunt new territory.

Maybe it was because we'd made him leave those perfectly huntable birds, or maybe it was because he was just incorrigible, but Gus went quickly back to his old ways. He busted a couple of coveys, ran out so far ahead he could have been a cavalry scout, and generally behaved like the worthless, hardheaded, no-account sonofabitch my partner started, once again, reminding him he was.

Still, we hunted on, until late afternoon when the ricebirds flocked overhead and we heard the occasional owl, doing a *who-cooks-for-you* down in the gum swamps. Then, with less than twenty minutes of hunting time left in the day, the Dr. Jekyll side of Gus's deeply split personality resurfaced and he pointed another covey like a pro. Held while we made the flush. Then pointed two or three singles. He did not retrieve our downed birds, but only because we beat him to them.

Except for the smell, he was a delight.

"I'll *never* understand bird dogs," the man said wearily, when we got back to the car and loaded old Gus into the trunk. We smelled him all the way back to the farm where we dropped him off, unceremoniously, and he got his reward of a bowl of cold, dry food and a night locked up alone in a cold toolshed.

I wanted to pat the dog and tell him what good work he'd done—already, I remembered only the good parts—but I was dissuaded by the smell and by his owner's obvious belief that affection is purely wasted on a hardheaded pointer dog.

SIX

Hadley and I worked with Jeb every day, and he seemed to enjoy it almost as much as we did. He was, as they say, "plenty game." As the days went by, he got bigger and could, increasingly, run with real purpose instead of merely bounding in the aimless fashion of puppies. Now, he could decide where he wanted to be—the tree line at the edge of our meadow, most often—and his legs would take him there. Unfailingly and quickly.

Now and then, he would make a break for it, and it was all Hadley and I could do to run him down before he made it to the woods. I would shout for him to "Whoa!" Sometimes it worked, and, ominously, sometimes it did not. Jeb seemed to have worked it out in his mind that a command which could be immediately enforced had to be obeyed, but otherwise, all bets were off.

"I keep remembering what Winston told me at my birthday party," I said to Hadley one day after we'd managed to catch Jeb just before he reached the tree line.

"What's that?"

"He kept saying, 'That dog is going to run away on you.'"

"Do you think he will, Dad?"

"Seems like he wants to."

"I wonder why."

Her Lab had never strayed very far from home, even when she was a pup, and I imagine that Hadley believed it was because the dog felt no need to leave home because home was so congenial. It was where she got fed and found plenty of affection. Why should Jeb want to run away when things were good at home, and when he had to understand that we wanted him to stick around?

"I think it's in a pointer's nature to want to run and hunt."

"No matter what?"

"I'm afraid so."

I told Hadley what I knew about pointers—from reading and from experience—and how, in the South, they liked to talk about "big-going dogs" that would "cover the country." I recalled some of my hunts with Gus.

"Well, that guy just sounds cruel to me," she said. "Like a real creep. If I was his dog, I'd run away, too. And do all that other stuff. Why was he so hard on the dog?"

"He wasn't that bad," I said. "There were people who were a lot harder on their dogs than he was." I told her about men who really did beat their dogs—beat them hard, out of angry violence and not just a desire to break them of some bad habit. They beat them because they were angry, and they took it out on the dog.

"That's sick," Hadley said.

"Maybe," I said. "But some men did worse. You'd hear stories about men who would shoot their dogs."

"*Really?*"

"Afraid so."

"*Why?*"

"Well, I suppose they'd do it when they had a dog running out of control, flushing birds wild or chasing deer or something like that. They couldn't get the dog's attention by yelling, and there was no way they were ever going to be able to run after the dog and catch it. So, they would wait until the dog was just barely in shotgun range and then shoot so that the pellets would sting and hurt when they hit, but wouldn't break the skin and really injure the dog. That was probably the idea, anyway. I imagine some dogs were injured."

"And probably some of them were killed," she said furiously. "Or had their eyes put out."

"I imagine."

"That's really sick. I think people like that should go to jail."

I didn't think much of them, either, I said. Which was true, these days. But when I'd been about her age, and a little older, I'd seen enough of the other kind of attitude to be, at least, ambivalent. After hunting with old Gus and other dogs like him, I, too, had begun to think that maybe pointers were incorrigible and did not respond to affection and positive reinforcement. Maybe they were the canine equivalent of mules, bred for hard work so that kindness and love was wasted on them. Gus's owner was never really brutal. If he ever raised his hand against the dog, it wasn't with any real force. He wasn't trying to inflict pain. And, anyway, it would have taken a lot to hurt old Gus. Like all the other pointers of my early experience, he was a true stoic in that regard.

One day when we had him out by a place that had been long abandoned by some hard-luck sharecropper, Gus stepped on a piece of broken glass and cut his pad deeply. We didn't see it happen and didn't find the glass shard until later, when we went back to look for it. Gus was way out ahead of us, as usual, and we noticed he was limping.

"Must have picked up a thorn or something," the man said. "I'll take it out if the old fool ever comes close enough for me to get ahold of him."

We kept watching Gus; he had a pretty pronounced limp. Bad enough to actually slow him down some so that we were eventually able to close the distance between us without running. And when we got closer, we could see the dog's brisket was red with blood.

"Oh, man. Whoa, Gus," the man said, with real concern in his voice.

Gus wasn't doing "Whoa" that day—or most other days, for that matter—so it was a while before we finally got close enough to separate and circle him. After a little bit, we had him boxed in and he just stopped running and looked at us, kind of bewildered. We closed in and caught him. I held the dog down while the man looked him over.

"Oh, buddy," he said, "you really done it to yourself this time."

There was so much blood that we couldn't tell how deep the cut was—but it was clearly very bad. Gus didn't seem to be in any pain. He wasn't moaning or anything. The man took out a bandana and wrapped it around Gus's paw and knotted it. And when he finished and was wiping his bloody hands off on his pants, Gus got up on his feet and tried to take off and start hunting. We had to catch him again and rewrap his bloody paw with the bandana.

"Here," the man said, "you carry the guns. Unload them, first."

I did this while he held Gus.

When I had an unloaded gun under each arm, the man picked Gus up and lifted him over his head and rested him on his shoulders in what the Boy Scouts taught as a "fireman's carry."

Strangely, Gus did not resist.

"Okay," the man said. "Now let's get him back to the car and see if we can find him a vet somewhere."

It was a half-mile walk, anyway, and before we'd gone very far, the bandana had worked its way off Gus's paw. The cut was still bleeding, and by the time we got back to the car, both man and dog were covered with blood.

The man didn't seem to notice, or mind, anyway; merely kept saying things like, "Be easy, Gus. Just take it easy. We'll get you fixed, old buddy."

There were some old towels in the trunk where Gus usually rode, and we put them on the backseat, and for once, the dog rode inside with us when we went looking for a vet.

We found one who was at home on a Saturday morning, and he washed the cut and put antiseptic on it and bandaged it up. Gus would need a couple of weeks to heal, the vet said reassuringly, but he'd be fine. Standing there in his bloody hunting clothes, Gus's owner seemed exceedingly relieved. He thanked the vet, and we took Gus back to his quarters at the farm. On the way, the man stopped at the grocery store and picked up a half a pound of hamburger as a treat for Gus.

"He's lost so much blood, you know," the man said sheepishly, like he wanted me to understand he wasn't turning soft on me; that there was a sound medical reason—not some kind of sappy sentiment—behind feeding old Gus a little chopped beef instead of the usual dry cereal when he got home that night.

I might have been young, but I saw right through that one.

I told Hadley that story because it had made such an impression on me when I was about her age, and because I wanted her to understand something I had tumbled to that day.

My insight, if you could call it that, was this: While there were hunters who really didn't like their dogs and treated them in a fashion that was borderline sadistic (and sometimes crossed the border), a lot of them felt a kind of pride in their dogs' unbiddable and unbreakable spirit. They believed that pointers were supposed to be big-going, hard-headed, unpredictable, and close to impossible to control. They might have said they wanted a dog that was perfectly and instantly obedient to every command; that didn't head for the county line as soon as you turned him loose to hunt; didn't chase deer; didn't roll in dead things; didn't bust coveys; didn't occasionally eat a bird he'd been sent out to retrieve; didn't do any of the hundred and one things that drove bird hunters crazy about their dogs, and that they bitched about with such relish.

But they were lying. Or maybe "dissembling" is the better, more charitable word.

It wasn't that they were too lazy to work with a dog and train him up to something close to perfection—though this was certainly true of the worst of them, especially the ones who did resort to brutality. The fact is, they believed that a civilian pointer—as opposed to the professionals that ran field trials or were part of some rich plantation owner's string of dogs—was by nature ornery and high-spirited and inclined to go his own way and do whatever the hell he got it in his mind to do at the time, and damn the consequences.

They secretly admired these things in a dog, and believed that if things were turned around and they were dogs themselves, they would have been exactly the same way, if not worse.

The men who would take me hunting back then were good family types who had left their wild, youthful days behind them and, truth be told, probably hadn't been that rambunctious, even then. Maybe they liked to think that just under the skin of an insurance man, there existed the heart of a hard-riding Confederate cavalry trooper like some imagined ancestor.

The more I hunted with men like these, the more I realized that when they told stories about their dogs—something they plainly enjoyed doing—they were more apt to talk about episodes where the dog had behaved badly than when he had performed well. The best stories were always the funniest stories, and in them, the dog was always doing something that drove his owner crazy.

"Let me tell you what that rock-brained, road-running fool of mine did to me . . . " one of these tales would begin, and I'd listen raptly.

Dog owners, they say, like to see themselves reflected in the personality and breeding of their dogs. A Park Avenue lady of elegance and sophistication chooses a manicured poodle (which was once actually a fine hunting breed) because she likes the dog's poise and refinement. The dog's virtues are those that she imagines, desires, and cultivates in herself. Lab owners of my experience—whether they are hunters or not—tend to be gregarious, friendly, affable people. Just like their dogs. And people who own Rhodesian ridgebacks and Dobermans tend to view the world with a measure of suspicion, if not hostility.

The rule is, of course, elastic. But among the bird hunters of my early acquaintance, you saw a distinct sympathy for the kind of dog that had the talent and the moves mixed with a certain unpredictability and plain ornery unwillingness to stick to the rules; like the kid in school who always drove the teachers crazy. They knew he had the mind for the work if they could ever just get him to settle down and concentrate.

The rule held even for the men I knew who had pretty good dogs. Some of them had trained the dogs themselves, and some had even sent them off to professionals who sent them back trained up so they would respond to hand signals and stand steady to wing and shot. This kind of perfection quickly slipped. It required too much reinforcement, and the kind of men I went out with wanted to hunt. They weren't inclined to stop everything in the field and correct a dog when he made a mistake. They would just yell and cuss and keep on hunting. Gradually, the dog would forget the intricacies of his training even if he was still, essentially, a good and reliable hunter.

An uncle of mine, named Robin, had a pair of pointers that he bought from a reputable breeder and sent to a trainer when they were two years old. The dogs were big and rangy, and he named them Buck and Bandit. This, too, was typical of pointer owners. They liked hard, one- or two-syllable country-boy names for their dogs. Somebody once told me that any name was good for a pointer as long as it rolled off the tongue easily in combination with "goddammit."

Anyway . . . Buck and Bandit were the first really good pointers I'd ever hunted with, and if my uncle invited me, I went. No matter what.

They ran big, like pointers are supposed to do. But Buck and Bandit had a way of working in tandem. They would course through the broomweed and briars on long casts, checking themselves and looking back to Robin every now and then to make sure they weren't too far out. We almost always had them in view.

They also looked out for each other and seldom poached the other dog's territory. And, best of all, when one of them hit a point and the other dog saw it, he would stop, too, and back the point. One dog on birds and the other backing was just about the prettiest sight you could see when you were hunting quail. There was just something so resolute about it. You wanted a camera whenever it happened.

But good as they were, Buck and Bandit were not perfect. They still had their Mr. Hyde moments when they would bust coveys and then go off after the singles. Sometimes they would just say, "The hell with it, I'll take the yelling and the spanking," and take off after a deer. They would, of course, roll in anything dead that they had the good fortune to find.

One thing I never saw them do, however, was simply run away and stay gone, the way other pointers of my acquaintance had.

I said something about this, once, to Robin.

"Well, you're right about that," Robin said. "But they sure did it before I sent 'em away to get trained. I had a guard from the prison road crew call me one day and tell me he'd found those dogs a good five miles from where I'd last seen them. I just hope you haven't put the hex on me, mentioning it like that."

They didn't run away that day, or any other time I hunted with them.

Still, they were pointers, and while you can suppress the urge through training, you can never really eliminate it.

"Let me tell you about those dogs of mine," Robin said to me one day after I hadn't seen him, or hunted with him for a while.

I thought he was going to brag on them for some nice piece of work. But, like I say, those aren't the stories the bird hunters I knew liked to tell on their dogs.

"Couple of weeks ago," he started, "it was a beautiful Saturday morning, and I just had to get out. Trouble was, I had a wedding to go to that afternoon, and your aunt Frances told me that if I was late for it, she was going to kill me. Slowly and painfully.

"I told her there was nothing to worry about. I just wanted to get out for a couple of hours, check out a place close to home. I'd be back in plenty of time to change and make the wedding. So I loaded up the dogs and went off, and they were into birds almost as soon as they hit the ground.

"We hunted that covey and then another, and I wasn't even half a mile from the car. I've never seen those dogs hunt better. They were backing like champions, and I don't believe they missed a single. Never been prouder of those two.

"Things were so good that I naturally lost track of time. When I finally looked at my watch, I saw I was cutting it pretty thin. But the dogs were right out ahead of me and we were still pretty close to the truck. I figured if I called 'em in and loaded up, right then, I could make it back in time . . . just barely.

"So I called to 'em. 'Buck, Bandit, let's go. Kennel up.'

"Those dogs stopped what they were doing and they looked back at me. Then they looked at each other. Then they looked around at all that fine-looking bird country they hadn't hunted yet. Checked the sky for rain, and saw the sun was out and still had a long way to go before it set.

"Then, they looked at each other again and I'll swear that this time, you could see this look pass between them. It was like they were saying to each other, 'Quit? Quit *now*? Hell, we're just getting started, and this weenie wants to quit and go home. Well, no thank you, Mr. Boss Man, believe we'll just keep on hunting. You can come along if you want to.'

"And then I saw their hindquarters, heading over the hill and making for the county line. I yelled and I yelled and they never broke stride and they never looked back."

"What did you do?" I asked.

"For a while," he said, "I just stood there feeling stupid. When that didn't accomplish anything, I walked back to the truck, drove home, changed clothes, and went to the wedding. I made an appearance at the reception. Drank some punch, told the bride how lovely she looked, then ducked out and drove back to the woods to where I'd last seen Buck and Bandit. I parked and got out, walked a little ways into the woods, still wearing my Sunday School clothes, called one time, and here they came. I couldn't do anything except tell 'em to 'Kennel up.' You don't punish a dog after he's come in. That just makes it harder to get him to come in the next time. They got away clean.

"Those dogs *knew*, I'm telling you, son. All the times I'd had them out, this was the one when they knew they could take off and there was no chance I'd be coming after them."

Robin liked that story. I heard him tell it again and again, and it seemed to get better every time.

Hadley liked it too. Robin was still living then, and he was one of her favorite relatives. She could imagine him telling the story and that made it good. But it was the dog angle that really got her. The way those pointers had picked the absolute *worst* time to run away—from Robin's point of view, anyway. In their estimation, there couldn't have been a better time for a jailbreak.

"Do you think Jeb will be like that, Dad?" Hadley said.

"I don't know. Probably. And you know what?"

"What?"

"I actually kind of hope so."

Be careful, they say, what you wish for, because you just might get it. And in my case, Jeb made sure I got it. Good and hard.

But that came later.

SEVEN

In those first few weeks, the bonding between man and dog that the books talked about was, undeniably, happening. And not just on one side, either. If Jeb seemed to think of me as his companion and to feel like things were somehow not right when we weren't in each other's company—well, I was experiencing something very similar. I had been fond of Molly, my Brittany, and she seemed to think I was okay since I was the one who took her hunting and who fed her. But, she was somewhat aloof as dogs go, and even a little cold. She didn't crave affection—not like Hadley's Lab, certainly—and she didn't mind being alone somewhere in the house when there were people around. Molly had been closer to my daughters than she'd ever been to me and, in truth, she hadn't been a real strong people dog.

I'd expected more of the same from Jeb. For one thing, I'd assumed that Molly's distant and remote attitude was part of any hunting dog's personality. These breeds, I reasoned, were bred to find game and handle themselves in the field and, so, they would necessarily be short on the domestic skills. And, then, there were those pointers I'd known as a kid; those tough dogs that had been neglected—at best—by their owners. They seemed to believe that any relationship they had with a human was one of pure necessity, with no room for the softer emotions.

Pointers, according to what I'd always been told, did not make good house dogs or pets. The best you could hope for, then, was a dog that would be inconspicuous and obedient. If you wanted affection and companionship, then you needed to get yourself a Lab.

Jeb, however, did not seem to fit my preconceptions. Not at all.

For one thing, when he was in the house, he liked being where the people were. He would sit down in front of you and look up at you in this eager, expectant sort of way. You would need a heart of the coldest stone not to reach down and give him a few pats or rub his ears and scratch his brisket. And when you did, he seemed to really appreciate it. So you got some good feedback. Jeb wasn't one of those one-way pups. It wasn't all about him.

In fact, if you were sitting in a chair, after you'd rubbed his ears and patted his head, he would slowly work his way up into your lap. He was still a puppy when he started with this act, and it was undeniably cute. Everyone in the family seemed to think so, anyway. And so did most of the people who came by to visit or eat dinner. There were, of course, exceptions. Ladies in nice dresses seemed a little put off by Jeb's advances. He was a short-haired dog, but he did shed a little, and his coat was mostly white. Dog hair doesn't do much for a black party dress. And, then, there were some people who just didn't like the idea of a dog—even one that was still mostly puppy—parking himself in their laps. Something to do with dignity, I expect, and the proper order of things.

To their way of thinking, dogs and other animals, if they were allowed inside at all, were supposed to keep all four paws on the floor.

I had my own reservations about this act of Jeb's. I didn't have any hard-and-fast rules about how many paws an animal needed to keep on the floor or anything like that, but in my years of dreaming about pointers, I'd never imagined one as a lap dog. My vision was of big-going dogs, oblivious to pain and the blandishments of the soft, nonhunting life. I was beginning to worry that, with Jeb, what I had on my hands was a lover, not a hunter.

Still, I couldn't resist when he crawled up into my lap and, after I'd rubbed his ears and neck for a few minutes, went to sleep. My wife and daughters were also suckers for that act.

There were other ways in which I was turning soft on this dog that I had once imagined as my tough-guy sidekick in the bird covers. He rode with me, everywhere I went, and he still spent the working day with me at the office. I gave him treats, table scraps and the like, and generally pampered him in ways that the pointer owners I'd known as a boy would have thought foolish, and guaranteed to turn a good bird dog into a spoiled, no-account pet.

I may have worried about this; but not very much. And, anyway, I couldn't help myself. Dogs have a way of insinuating themselves into the lives of the families they come to live with, and if they live inside, and there are kids around, things tend to work out in their favor. How they do this is a mystery going back to those ancient days when the first dog came into some human camp, close to the fire, and cadged a little food. Dogs can be taught a lot of specialized skills—including pointing and retrieving birds—but all of them are born knowing one thing, and that is how to make themselves appealing to humans. It is an evolutionary triumph that I, for one, am grateful for.

Meanwhile . . . Jeb was not a puppy any longer, and just when his training needed to be getting more serious, I started letting it slide. My work had me on the road for days (and sometimes, weeks) at a time, and as winter settled in, Hadley was leaving for school on the bus when it was barely daylight and coming home after dark. Winter came on hard, the way it does in Vermont, and there was too much snow on the ground to do much training, even on the weekends when I was at home.

I told myself that I'd pick up where we'd left off in the spring, when the ground dried out. By then, though, Jeb was nearly a year old and the game had changed. For one thing, there was no way I could run him down and catch him if he didn't come when called. If I wanted to control him, it had to be on a lead. When I put him on one, he seemed calm and responsive. Then, when I released him, he put his ears back and lit out for the territories. I might not see him again for an hour.

When he returned after one of these rambles, I would shake a finger in his face and tell him he was a bad boy, and he would give me a look of sincere contrition. Then, next day, same thing.

I bought a long lead with a choke collar on the end so that he could run out some thirty yards ahead of me and then, if he didn't turn and come back when I called, I could put some pressure on him and stop him. I picked that system up, no doubt, from one of the many books on dog training I had acquired.

I expected immediate results and I got them. Jeb would run out to the end of the lead, and when he came to the end and the choke collar started to cut off his air, instead of turning, he would sit down. When I pulled on the lead to try to bring him in, he would resist to the point of near strangulation. This went on for a couple of weeks until, eventually, Jeb would either stand at my heel when I put the lead and the collar on him, or charge out until he'd taken up all the slack, and then, sit down and refuse to move.

I kept trying, and this was one of many mistakes I made in those early, frustrating training sessions. I didn't really know what I was doing, but that wasn't an insurmountable problem. After all, I had the books, and I knew people who owned bird dogs and had some of their own ideas about training them. I was never short on advice.

But I suffered, as a dog trainer, from a severe deficit in temperament: I lacked the vital ingredient of patience.

Some of this was just my nature, and some was the by-product of a typically too-busy, overstressed life—work, travel, kids in school, and the other, routine obligations of adulthood.

I knew dog people who never seemed to lose it when they were working with a dog. They could be firm without being harsh, and they could take it in stride when the dog made a mistake. They didn't expect perfection, so they weren't disappointed when they didn't get it. But, it seemed, these lowered (and, perhaps, more realistic) expectations seemed to produce better results.

I, on the other hand, got less and less the more I expected. And when I didn't get it, I got irritated and then frustrated and then angry. I would find myself yelling at Jeb and then shaking my finger in his face and, finally, using more force than necessary when I was trying to correct him. I didn't beat him, but I certainly grabbed him more violently than I needed to. He never yelped or howled when I did it. He would merely stand stoically where I had put him, looking at me with what I would have sworn was an expression that blended betrayal and hurt. *How could you?* he seemed to be saying reproachfully. *I thought we were buddies.*

I'm told that dogs do not make facial expressions, and maybe they don't. Perhaps I was merely projecting, seeing what I thought should have been the dog's expression. But whether I saw it or merely imagined that I did, the expression on Jeb's face filled me with shame and regret, and I would wonder, sometimes, if I might be edging over to the kind of hard, brutal discipline used by those men I'd known in my youth.

I knew I didn't want that. Would rather not hunt with Jeb than go that route.

So, after I'd lost my temper and the dog would be looking up at me with fear in his eyes, I would sigh and say, "Come on, bud. Let's go home."

And we would trudge back to the house with me now trying to make Jeb obey the command "Heel."

He didn't get that one, either. So he would either strain at the leash or sit down until I had to force him to stand and walk.

I would return to the house in a state of utter frustration.

"We'll try again tomorrow," I'd say while I stored my training tools. Jeb would look at me like he understood what I was saying, and dreaded it.

"You'll get it, bud. I know you will. You're a smart dog. Question is . . . do you have a smart owner?"

In my imagination, Jeb's expression and body language said, emphatically, "Not hardly."

We stayed at it all through spring and into summer, and didn't have much to show for it except an increasingly strained relationship. I was discouraged and frustrated. Jeb, I think, was alternately defiant and bewildered.

Now and then, in one of our sessions, I would try something new. I'd read somewhere that you want to make the training fun for the dog, and keep things as low-key as possible. So I thought that maybe Jeb would feel under less pressure if I let him off the lead after we had been at it for a while. This demonstration of just how much I trusted him, I reasoned, might influence him. Perhaps he would think that he needed to make some kind of reciprocal gesture. Like, for instance, sticking around and doing what I was trying to teach him to do.

So I knelt down next to him and stroked his flank with one hand while I unclipped the lead from his collar with the other.

"Good man," I said soothingly, "you're a good man. Just hold what you got. Steady, Jeb. Stand steady for me, buddy."

I stood and he looked up at me. There was puzzlement in his eyes. He didn't quite get it. Wasn't sure what was coming next. He stood there, waiting.

Then, I would swear in court, I could see the realization in his eyes—he was off that hateful lead and I was just far enough away that if he made a break, there was no way I could grab him. He was looking at a clean getaway with the woods no more than a hundred yards away. After that . . . freedom. Dogs run down fugitive men all the time. But no fugitive dog has ever been run down by a man.

It happened quickly. His nostrils flared and his front legs stretched out and in about ten feet, he was in full stride.

"*Jeb!*"

There was nothing but futility in that command. He hit the tree line going full bore and never looked back. I hollered for him again, knowing that it was pointless. I may have had some notion that by yelling at him to come back, I was letting him know that this was not what schoolteachers like to call "acceptable behavior."

I coiled the lead and trudged home. Jeb returned three or four hours later with a wild look in his eye, his mouth frothy, and a layer of black mud on his belly.

I let him in without a word. He might have been my teenage son, returning the family car several hours late.

Hadley offered to help, and I now wish devoutly that I had taken her up on the offer. I told myself that I turned her down because she was a busy young girl with better things to do than help her stubborn old man train a pigheaded dog. But that was false magnanimity. The shameful truth is that I was too proud to take help. I wanted to be able to say that I had trained my dog myself, and that the result was a cool, confident, efficient bird-hunting team, each member anticipating the other's moves and needs so that the communication between them was silent and flawless.

I was in the grip of that old corrupter, pride—and too proud to admit it. Men compete at everything. I imagined some of my hunting buddies, who had dogs of their own, going out with me and admiring my dog's performance—a dog I had trained myself—even if they couldn't admit it. And once I had established that goal, there was no way I could back off of it and admit failure. If I understood this at the time, I kept that knowledge very deeply buried and soldiered on, no doubt doing more harm than good. The real shame was, what should have been a good, satisfying time spent with my dog became an ordeal for both of us. I realized what I'd missed when I watched Hadley training her Lab: in a nutshell, how much *fun* she was having. How the thing itself was the point.

She probably would have helped me see this, but I was locked into my solitary quest and steadily losing ground.

◆

At some point, I told myself that there probably wouldn't be any progress until Jeb could get into the field and actually gain some experience on real birds. One friend who hunted a lot and was successful had said to me, "Dogs train themselves. After they've been around birds for a while, they figure it out."

Considering that remark, many years later, I now think he was on to something. But I also realize that he was not speaking literally. Dogs learn a lot in the field, through experience, the best teacher of all. But they need to have learned the fundamentals first. A dog certainly does not learn anything by running flat out through the woods chasing everything he sees or smells, whether it has feathers or fur.

But in my desperation, I took the remark literally. Jeb and I had just enough communication and had actually put together a sufficient number of passable training sessions that I convinced myself the truth would be revealed to him, once we were in the field together, hunting birds. I backed off on the lawn training, which was getting nowhere, anyway. I still kept him close, so he rode with me in the truck and went with me to the office. I wanted him to feel like he needed that proximity. That, I thought, would keep him close—reasonably close, anyway—when we were in the field.

He'd miss me, I thought, if he got too far out. And he would come back to his companion.

EIGHT

Opening day seemed to arrive, as it usually does, both too early and too late. Too early, because the last Saturday in September—the traditional opening day for grouse in Vermont—can be hot, and most of the leaves will still be on the trees. Both dogs and hunters tire in the heat, and when a bird flushes, while you might hear him, you seldom see even a feather in the dense foliage. It is frustrating, and you long for the crisp days of late October when the air is cool and the trees are bare.

But, opening day also seems late because you have been waiting for it to arrive through the pointless days of late summer when there isn't much going on in the way of sport (unless you hunt either bears or squirrels, which come into season in early September). By August, the rivers are down and the trout fishing has slowed. There is some smallmouth fishing in the larger streams, but even that has a sluggish, desultory quality. On the whole, from about mid-July on, you'd rather be hunting birds.

Thursday before opening day, I performed my annual bird-hunting devotionals. I greased my boots, wiped the excess oil off my shotgun, sorted through the loose shells left over from last season, and took my briarproofs and vest out of the trunk where I had stored them at the end of last season. They smelled musty and a little rank, especially the vest.

There were a couple of bloodstains around the game bag, and a few vagrant feathers drifted through the room when I opened it.

I bought a license and on Friday night, I talked to a couple of friends to make sure we wouldn't be hunting the same places. We had to be a little imprecise about exactly where we would be going. You like to keep the location of your best bird coverts secret, so you merely say you will be hunting north of here and west of there, or something equally vague.

The people I talked to seemed to think we were in for a good season. Everyone was seeing—or hearing, anyway—a lot of birds. I went to sleep eager, but also feeling qualms about Jeb. I realized that my attempt at training him had been a woeful failure, and in the small, coldly realistic portion of my brain, I knew that it was likely to be a frustrating, if not maddening, opening day.

Still . . . we live on hope. I told myself not to expect too much from Jeb, not to lose my temper but to make it fun for him to be in the woods with me, to make sure that he realized that we were in this thing together. And so on, until I fell asleep.

I ate soft eggs and crisp bacon for breakfast, drank a cup of strong coffee, and poured the rest of the pot into the thermos I'd been using for years. Checked my vest for the third or fourth time, and found it still held everything I needed.

"Come on, bud," I said. "Let's go hunting."

Jeb sat up proud and eager in the front seat of my truck, and I imagined that he knew what this trip was about and that he was determined to distinguish himself in the field. There is no limit to the capacity of a certain kind of bird hunter to anthropomorphize his dog's every action and posture. I had established this specific idea of Jeb's character in my mind. He was colorful but dutiful; impulsive but talented; a hard charger who took care of business . . . and so on. All absurd, of course. In truth, he was a young, energetic, poorly trained pointer, and he didn't have any idea where we were going or why. He was what he was.

As for me . . . I was a fool.

I dropped down into four-wheel drive and took an old, badly rutted logging road that climbed up a hillside to a long ridge. The road ran through a stand of mature hardwoods that wouldn't have drawn the attention of any bird hunter scouting for new territory. But the ridge flattened out at the top and had been farmed for years and years. Then, like a lot of other struggling Vermont farmers, the owner of this place just gave up and let it go back. The trees in the old orchard hadn't been pruned or sprayed for a decade or more, but they still bore apples that were gnarled and spotted and generally unappealing in their appearance, though the grouse and deer feasted on them.

The old cleared fields on the hilltop were now covered with aspen trees, briars, thorn apples, and other things that grouse liked, and the wet spots were thick with alders and later in the season, you could find woodcock there. This hillside covert was my prime hunting territory. Molly and I had made a living off the place for five years, and now, I told myself, it was Jeb's turn.

I parked next to the ruins of an old farm shed, complete with a rusting, derelict car body, and let Jeb out of the truck.

"Okay, buddy. Showtime."

Jeb jumped out of the truck and stood on the unfamiliar ground, blinking. He looked around and sniffed the air. Marked a bush. Looked at me and waited, sort of expectantly, to see just what it was I had in mind.

I took his collar off and replaced it with one that had a small, copper bell attached. This is the traditional way of keeping track of a bird dog in the thick New England coverts. As long as the dog is moving, you can hear the bell. Provided, that is, that the dog is within hearing range, and that is a very large qualifier. But if the dog is hunting close, when you no longer hear the bell, you can assume he is on point. Then, you walk carefully but briskly toward the area where you last heard the bell, with your gun ready in case the bird flushes before you see the dog on point. The system has worked for thousands of bird hunter/bird dog teams. Molly and I had used it very effectively. There were electronic beeper collars coming along, but I resisted them.

It would not be long before I would grasp at any new gizmo that promised to make a bird dog perform, but today I was thinking "no gimmicks" as I buckled the collar around Jeb's neck. We were going to "stay with the old paths," as one of my favorite Bible passages instructs us.

Jeb wasn't sure about that bell. He took a few steps and the ringing seemed to confuse him.

"It's okay, bud. Go hunt birds."

He stared back at me with a look that I took for uncertainty. So I waved my hand at him, indicating that I wanted him to stretch his legs. Get out there and cruise the country.

Never has a request been so enthusiastically granted. It was almost as though Jeb's mind formulated the thing this way: "Okay, Boss Man. You want me to move out. I'll show you some moving out. You ain't seen moving out like the moving out you are fixing to see."

He started running, and after the first dozen strides or so, he put it into overdrive. He was running like Seabiscuit on the backstretch, opening it up and leaving the field in his dust.

"Well," I thought, "I'll never have to worry about him being underfoot."

I watched him cover a patch of open ground—one hundred yards, maybe—and then disappear into a thick stand of thorn apples. I could still hear the bell. Faintly. Ever so faintly. And then . . . I couldn't hear the bell or see my dog.

"Jeb," I hollered forlornly, waiting for him to reappear. I might have been waiting, still, if I hadn't admitted to myself that he wasn't going to be passing this way again for a while—maybe not until he had lapped the whole ridgeline—and that maybe I'd better start walking after him. Who knew; we might bump into each other by accident somewhere on the ridgeline. I might even find him staunch on point. (I was still entertaining some delusions of that sort.)

So I put the gun on my shoulder and started across the open ground toward the place where I had last seen my highballing bird dog. This wasn't quite the way I'd imagined it, but as I told myself, it was still early in both the season and Jeb's hunting career. Things had to get better.

Didn't they?

Not that day, they didn't. For at least two full hours, I wandered through my favorite covert occasionally catching sight of my dog—a flash of white in the leaves and undergrowth—sometimes hearing his bell, and always in a state of frustration. For a while, I yelled at him to "Come." I might just as well have been yelling to the heavens for world peace.

It would have been a pleasant walk if I had been alone. I had hunted places like this without a dog during the first few years of my time in Vermont. It was a fairly straightforward proposition: You pushed briskly through the brush because you wanted to cover as much ground as possible, and you wanted to be on top of the birds before they would run away or flush out of range. There was nothing stealthy, then, about the way you moved, and it was slightly counterintuitive that way. But I got used to it and had some success.

But once I had started hunting with dogs—other hunters' dogs at first, and, then, my own—I told myself that this was the sovereign way. The dog could cover so much more ground, for one thing, so you could slow it down. Also, the dog could slither into the places that were tight with branches or thick with briars, so you didn't have to get cut up trying to get a tight-holding bird to flush. On one memorable occasion when I'd been hunting without a dog, I'd stepped on a tangle of blackberry vines and one of them had sprung up and slapped me in the face, driving one of the thorns right into my eye.

The thorn broke off and stayed in my eye (the white part, mercifully), and I managed to stumble out of the woods and back to my truck. I drove to my doctor's house, since it was a Saturday and he wasn't keeping office hours. Luckily, he did have some instruments and medicines at home, so he was able to wash my eye out with something that numbed it and then pull the thorn out with tweezers. I had to wear a patch for a couple of days. Still, I felt like I'd gotten off easy.

Hunting with a dog made this sort of thing a lot less likely. Also, if you had a good dog, you would probably flush more birds than you would if hunting by yourself. Going with a dog was a less strenuous and generally more productive way to hunt, then, which would be enough to close the deal right there. But there was a bonus, I'd discovered.

Namely, watching the dog work.

Before I started hunting with my own dog, I'd hear veteran bird hunters say, "It isn't the birds that keep me going out; it's the dog work," and I would discount those words the way you do when some angler tells you, after a fishless day, "It doesn't matter if I don't catch anything; I just like to get out."

But after a while, you recognize the seed of truth there. The dog work becomes, if not the *only* element of the game, then certainly, the most seductive. The flush and the shot are still necessary, but no longer sufficient. Once you've gotten used to hunting grouse with a good dog, the experience is distinctly impoverished when you go out alone.

But . . . the qualifier is exceedingly important. While hunting with a good dog raises the quality of the thing, hunting—if it can be called that—with an untrained, unbiddable, out-of-control dog . . . well, that sours the thing, and you start to think about giving it up. Or going back, anyway, to doing it on your own, even if it means getting slapped in the face now and then by briars. I was feeling that way as I trudged through my favorite covert, alternately pleading with Jeb to come in and hunt with me and threatening him with mayhem if he didn't.

Neither worked.

I flushed a bird, on my own, and was too surprised to get the gun up. And, anyway, I never really had a shot, catching just the slightest glimpse of the bird through a break in the foliage.

I wondered how many Jeb had put up. And, if he had, what his re-action had been.

I plucked one of the less deformed and blemished apples from a tree in the old orchard and sat on a blowdown to eat it. It was firm and tart, and I picked two more and put them in my game bag for later. Not much chance, I thought, that they would be sharing space with any grouse.

I made my way back to the truck, and, eventually, Jeb did too, lathered and frantic.

"Kennel up," I said.

I'd found the one command he would instantly obey. He jumped eagerly into the cab of the truck. No show of remorse.

"So that's how it's going to be?" I said.

We went to a few other places that day, and it was more of the same. I heard another bird or two but never got a shot. I have no idea what sort of adventures Jeb may have had on his long walkabouts through my favorite coverts. I assume he also put up a bird or two. How he responded to the experience remains a mystery. At the end of the day, we were both tired, and one of us, anyway, was exceedingly discouraged.

Not long after we got home, while Jeb was eating his supper and I was consoling myself with a beer, the phone rang. It was one of my bird-hunting acquaintances. During the season, the tom-toms beat more or less constantly, carrying news of the hunt. This news is slightly more trustworthy than what you hear on the networks, and a lot more entertaining.

"So," my friend Bill said, "how did you and that greyhound make out?"

"Not bad," I said, trying to sound as poised as Dan Rather.

"You kill some birds, then?"

"Ah . . . no. We didn't exactly put any on the ground."

"But you found some?"

"Oh, yes."

"Great. How about the dog? He make some good points?"

"Well, he's still a little young," I said. Conversations between sportsmen are filled with evasions.

"But he worked all right?"

"He's coming along," I said, and changed the subject.

"How about you? How did you make out?"

"We had a great day. Best opening day I can remember."

"Glad to hear it," I said, lying through my tightly clenched teeth. "You get your limit?"

"Not quite. Too many leaves. But Sherlock made eight good points. I got three."

"That's terrific," I said. "Way to go." No runner-up in a beauty contest has ever congratulated the winner with less sincerity.

"I think it's going to be a great season," Bill said. "You're in luck, bringing a new dog along in a year when there are plenty of birds. He'll get lots of practice."

"Absolutely," I said. "Couldn't have worked out better."

Practice, I thought, *for running a marathon.*

I listened indulgently while Bill told me the details of his day, and then hung up feeling not particularly guilty about my lies and evasions but very glum about the prospects for this bird season, and, probably, many more to come.

I opened another beer and looked over at Jeb, who had finished his dinner and gone to sleep on his beanbag bed. He was exhausted, and no surprise, there. No telling how many miles he'd run, flat out. At that moment, we were a picture of opposites. Jeb's belly was full and he was resting contentedly, while gloom hung over me like a bank of low, wet clouds.

I felt like the parent of a Little Leaguer who can't hit, catch, or throw, and has a neighbor whose son is a natural ballplayer. You try to keep the acids of envy, competition, and vanity from leaching into your sporting life and corrupting it; but this, it seems, is impossible.

Bird hunters, like Arab princes with their racehorses, take a kind of excessive pride in their dogs when they do well, as though this somehow brings glory and credit to them. Accordingly, if your dog does *not* do well—does as badly as Jeb had done on his first day in the field—then that brings shame down on you. Absurd, of course, but there it is. As much as I tried to tell myself that it wasn't a competition, I couldn't make the sale. I felt like there was a lot riding on Jeb's success in the field, and that I was backing a long shot.

NINE

Writing off a whole bird season seemed insupportable, so, even though I didn't have any reason to think Jeb would do better than he did on opening day, we went into the field again . . . and again. And, like they say, when you think that things can't get any worse, inevitably, they do. Jeb continued to run away and hunt—if you could call it that—on his own. I tried various remedies that I'd read about, including tying a fifty-foot lead to his collar and letting him drag that behind him, through the brush. The idea here was to slow him down, even if just a little, and to give me something to grab when I wanted to stop him. Provided, that is, I could get close enough to reach the lead. Hardly a sure thing.

But it did happen, and when it did, I would bring Jeb up short and he would fight against the lead until he had almost choked himself unconscious. And then, from time to time, he would get the lead tangled and bring himself up short out of my sight. When this happened, he would moan and bellow and carry on like he was being devoured by wild hogs or something, and I would run desperately through the woods until I got to him and released him.

This, of course, earned me no gratitude. As soon as I'd freed the tangle, Jeb would be off again, flat out. I finally gave up on the lead, figuring that it hadn't done any good and that Jeb might one day strangle himself on it.

Still, I held on to my hopes for Jeb, though I had no evidence to support them. I would tell myself that he was getting better, showing signs of interest, staying closer and coming, now and then, when called. But this was pure wishful thinking. I clung to the theory that bird dogs will eventually "train themselves." According to this theory, you merely need to spend enough time in the field with your dog and eventually, he will put it all together and begin to perform. It was a nice vision, but deep down, I didn't really believe it. We delude ourselves about many things—or try to, anyway.

There were days when I was sanguine about Jeb and walked along where I thought he had been, hoping to kick up a bird on my own and feeling the simple contentment that comes with being out in the woods. I told myself that I wasn't going to let some hardheaded hound ruin what had always been one of my deepest pleasures. And then, there were days when I believe I literally saw red, I was so frustrated and angry. A thin, crimson film would appear in front of my face, and I would find myself looking at the world through this filter. It was the color of rage. On those occasions, I understood exactly the motives of those men I remembered from my youth, beating on their dogs not to train them, discipline them, or correct them, but simply and purely to hurt them. Just to get even.

On those occasions, I honestly did take it personally; felt precisely like Jeb was doing it to me on purpose. I believed that he knew what he was supposed to do, and not doing it was defiance, pure and simple. It was a contest of wills, then, and I had to show him I had a stronger will than he. This was thoroughly irrational, of course, but by now I had come a long way down that road.

So, now and then, I'd catch up to him—with or without the lead— and I would hold him by the collar and push him to the ground. Using more force than was really necessary, I would keep him pinned while I shook my finger in his face and yelled at him to do whatever it was he hadn't done most recently. Usually I would yell *"Whoa, Jeb!"* over and over, as though sheer repetition would somehow get the command into the wiring so that he would respond to it in the future.

Didn't happen, though.

They say that it is a form of insanity to repeat some action, over and over, expecting a different result on the hundredth—or thousandth—try. By this measure, I was slowly going mad. And maybe not that slowly.

The arrival of the "flight birds"—migrating woodcock—changed things just enough to justify a little surge of optimism. When the flight birds are in, you generally find a lot of them in a small area. A few acres of young aspens or a patch of alders in a beaver swamp might hold ten or fifteen birds. Woodcock evidently put out a lot of scent, and they very seldom run when they are threatened. Instead, they hunker down and hold their ground, counting on their coloring (nearly perfect camouflage with a carpet of brown leaves) to protect them. When danger is too close, which can be a distance of less than a yard, they fly, with their primary feathers giving off a distinctive whistling sound.

So, if grouse are perhaps the most challenging bird—sometimes running, sometimes holding, often flushing out of range, and generally doing things to confound a hunting dog—woodcock might be considered the easiest. Dogs that do not have an especially good nose and therefore tend to crowd grouse before they smell them . . . these dogs often do fine with woodcock. They have no trouble smelling the birds, and the rest—hitting a point and holding it—is a matter of training.

Some years before Jeb became my hunting dog (and cross to bear), I'd talked to another Southerner who had found his way to Vermont, bringing a weakness for pointers with him. He'd told me that his dog— Flash, I believe, was the name; as in *The Alabama Flash*—"never did take to grouse." He suspected that "they're just too smart, and my old dog doesn't have the world's best nose."

But things were different, he went on, when it came to woodcock. "Old Flash, now, he can handle those stinky birds just fine. We both love it when the flight birds come through. He gets to be a real bird dog and I get to be a real hunter. He smells them just fine and he strikes a real pretty point—head kind of low to the ground and tail sticking up high in the air. I see him like that and it's almost like I'm back home, walking through a field of broomweed and briars. It's almost a surprise when just this one bird gets up, all wings and legs, flying kind of wonky, you know. But that's okay because the way they fly, even I can hit 'em. Yessir, when it comes to woodcock, me and the Flash are a pair of aces."

I wasn't sure about Jeb's nose. If he'd ever worked birds, I hadn't seen him do it. Could be he smelled them a long way, or, then again, maybe he didn't smell them at all. I'd never worked him on pigeons or released quail, and clearly, I should have. But, then, there were a lot of things I should have done with Jeb and hadn't.

About three weeks into the season, with most of the leaves now off the trees, we got a full moon and a cold front pushed through. Ideal conditions for inspiring the woodcock to begin their migration down from New Brunswick and other points north on their way to Louisiana. They fly at night and hunker down during the day, and on a crisp October morning after the wind had died and the sky had cleared, Jeb and I went into one of my favorite woodcock coverts.

I don't know what I was expecting. Probably not much. At best, I must have had a notion that I would kick up a few birds myself while Jeb cruised the country in his usual exuberant, undisciplined fashion. I was, in short, feeling philosophical. Conditioning myself, perhaps, to the idea of a ten-year binding contract with a dog that wouldn't hunt. Not with me, anyway.

I parked the truck and put Jeb on a short lead. As usual, he strained at it so hard that he almost choked himself.

"Take it easy, bud," I said, trying for a soothing, persuasive tone. "You'll get your chance." No response except, perhaps, to pull harder at the lead.

When we were at the edge of an aspen thicket, I let him off the lead.

"Now hunt close," I said. The futility of this command was beyond laughable.

Jeb started running, and he plainly had no plans on staying close. Then, about twenty yards out, he stopped.

In fact, he didn't merely stop. He went rigid. Locked up like a stone statue. His head was low to the ground and his tail was high and almost straight, which came as a surprise. I'd assumed that with his sickle tail, that wouldn't be possible. He was not holding a front paw up, the way bird dogs have been depicted so many times, but Jeb was clearly pointing something.

My dog, on point. Imagine.

"Whoa, Jeb," I said, without much conviction.

But he didn't move, so I started walking in on him. I could see he was quivering with anticipation and I knew that he was on the verge of rushing in on whatever it was he was scenting. And I was almost certain that it was a woodcock.

I walked faster.

"Easy, Jeb. Steady."

I had almost reached the spot where he was standing, when he couldn't hold himself back any longer. He broke and rushed in and the woodcock came up in a startling blur of feathers, making the trademark sound with its primaries. I didn't have a shot.

"Whoa, Jeb!" I shouted. But he was on the run, after the bird, and in a couple of seconds, he was out of sight.

But, damn, he *had* smelled the bird and, in a rudimentary fashion, he had pointed it, too. Hope surged inside me. Maybe, just maybe, if we kept doing this, he would get the idea that it was a partnership. That I was along for more than a walk and an occasional glimpse of my dog as he went rocketing by on his own private quest to stir up everything in the woods.

I started off in the direction he'd been traveling when I last saw him. If there was one bird, then there were probably others. Maybe he was on point again. I'd had a taste of what was possible, and now, I wanted more.

Didn't happen that day, though. I heard him put up a couple of other birds. He even barked at one. But I never got close enough to watch or to try and steady him. Still, when I finally got him back to the truck and loaded up, I felt more optimism than I had since before the season started.

"This thing might just work out, bud," I said.

He looked at me with that expression all dogs seem to have mastered—some combination of incomprehension and agreement. "Yeah, Boss," it says. "Whatever."

We had a couple of weeks to hunt the flight birds and I tried to take advantage of them. I went out after the working day was done and sometimes cut things short at the office. I was operating on the hope that exposure to a lot of birds would steady Jeb down and that maybe, just maybe, I could shoot a woodcock over one of his partial points and that when it happened, the lightbulb would go on over his head and he would say, "Oh. Yeah. So that's what this is all about."

He didn't do anything to make it easy for me. He ran with his customary vigor through the thick aspens and alders we hunted, and there was no way I could keep up with him. Being in close proximity to Jeb when he scented a bird was, I realized, going to be a matter of sheer dumb luck. And for days I felt a lot dumber than I did lucky.

Then, one day, it happened. He had run out ahead until he was tired of going in that direction, and then he turned around and came back on a slightly different course. I could hear him coming; he was still wearing the bell on his collar, though at his usual range, there was no way I could hear it.

But this time, I did. It was coincidence, but I wasn't complaining.

Then, the bell stopped, and when I took another couple of steps, I could see my dog, steady and pointing.

"Whoa, Jeb," I said. Just because it had never worked in the past, that was no reason to give up.

"Steady, Jeb."

I picked up the pace, hoping to get in gun range before that inevitable moment when he rushed the bird.

"Easy, buddy."

When I was ten or fifteen steps from Jeb, he plainly couldn't stand it any longer and broke. The bird came up, framed cleanly against the sky. I put the gun to my shoulder, covered the bird, and touched the trigger. The bird dropped cleanly.

It wasn't classic, but Jeb and I had our first kill.

TEN

That first bird had not exactly been a glorious triumph of man and dog. It was luck or an accident or providence. Much as I might have wanted to, I couldn't persuade myself that things were now different and that Jeb had suddenly found religion. At best, I could be grateful for two things: first, that Jeb hadn't been spooked by the sound of the gun. Some dogs are naturally gun-shy, and in my sorry attempt to train him, I'd never gotten him accustomed to the gun. And, then, Jeb hadn't charged in on the downed bird and eaten it. He merely ran on and was soon out of sight. As usual.

And that was the high point of that bird season.

When it was over, I put my gun up and stored my clothes and tried to console myself with easy rationalizations.

I hadn't worked enough with Jeb in the yard, I told myself, before the season began. An easy and obvious explanation that overlooked a couple of points. Namely, that I did not have infinite time and was on the road a lot, making my living. There was no consistency to my training attempts, however well-intentioned. And, then, even the successes that I did have—and the more dramatic ones that Hadley had worked—seemed to vanish when Jeb and I were in the field where he wouldn't obey *any* commands, *ever*.

And, then, there was the plain fact that he was still a very young dog. Just over a year old, barely a pup. I'd been told that some of the handlers at the big, opulent quail plantations down South didn't even start working with a dog until it was two years old, and then didn't expect it to be a field performer for another year or two. Trying to hunt birds—especially ruffed grouse—with a one-year-old dog was like trying to teach calculus to your grade-schooler. Unless you had a prodigy, it couldn't be done.

And, finally, when I was looking at things plainly, instead of through the wistful lens of hope, I would tell myself that maybe I just had one of those dogs that would never shape up and perform in the field. I had hunted with friends who had dogs like that, and had resigned themselves to walking through the woods never knowing where the dog was and then waiting, at the end of the day, for the dog to reappear and jump blithely in the truck, like everything was just Jake.

"He has his hunt," one of these men told me, "and I have mine. It's like a truce in one of those bad marriages. After a while you just stop fighting and you each go your own way."

And, I decided, I could live with that if I had to because, the thing was, I loved that dog, and so did my wife and my daughters. He had done that thing that dogs do best: he had insinuated himself into our lives.

Contrary to everything I'd been told when I was a kid, about how pointers do not make good house dogs and pets, how you should consider them working dogs and not much different from livestock, Jeb was a charmer and great fun to have around. He liked people—especially us—and he craved affection and returned it bountifully. If you were sitting in a chair, he would do his trick where he first sits at your feet to get his ears rubbed and then slowly works his way up into your lap. First one paw, then another, then his brisket, and, finally, his entire body, which was full grown now and quite a lapful. He seemed to think he was doing this very stealthily, too, as though if he took it by slow degrees, you wouldn't notice that here was this forty-five-pound dog (he was still small for the breed) lying across your lap. Then, after he'd been up there for a while, and decided it was safe and he wasn't going to be dumped back onto the floor, he would go to sleep.

Then, there were these endearing quirks of his. He had an especially comic routine built around feeding time. He seemed to know when his bowl was due to be filled, and when that time came, he would begin pacing and looking at his empty bowl and whimpering. When he'd finally gotten your attention and you picked up the bowl, he would bark and start turning in furious little circles as though the excitement was just too much and he couldn't stand it any longer.

"That's a helluva performance for a cup of dry cereal," a friend of mine said after he'd seen the show.

"You ought to see it when we add some bacon grease," I said. "He just about falls over in a swoon."

He played tug-of-war with Hadley's Lab, Tickle, who outweighed him two-to-one, each of them on the end of a knotted old bedsheet we left lying around for that purpose. The Lab seemed amused by the game, but Jeb took it seriously. He would drag the bedsheet over to Tickle where she was sleeping, then growl and paw the floor until she gave in and grabbed the other end and started tugging. Jeb would shake his head and try to get traction with his paws. It was an unequal contest, but he wouldn't quit. Finally, the Lab would get bored and drop her end of the sheet and Jeb would prance around the room like he was taking a victory lap, with the bedsheet—still in his mouth—as a trophy.

He often slept on his back with all four paws up in the air. He looked like one of those cartoon depictions of a dog that had been knocked unconscious, and you almost expected to see little stars in the air, over his head. He looked about as silly as it is possible for a dog to look, and we took countless pictures of Jeb in this posture.

All these things, and many more, endeared him to all of us, so we overlooked—or tried to—the features of his personality that were not so cute. And there were many.

Above all, he had a knack, a positively uncanny and unerring sense, for finding an open door, or for suddenly appearing at the door when you were leaving on an errand and slipping out past you on his way to what we called "a ramble."

Jeb was, in his soul, a rambling man. After a few hours (or less) indoors, he yearned to be out in the air and on the move. And he had a way of making it happen, no matter how careful we tried to be about keeping doors closed and not letting him get by us when we were on the way in or out.

When he took off on these jaunts, he might be gone for just a few minutes. More often, though, it was for a couple of hours. Now and then, he would stay gone all night long. We got complaints from people who lived a mile or two away and had dogs that were in heat. Would we *please* come get our dog and, in the future, keep him out of their yard and away from their dogs. We would apologize and tell ourselves that we'd have to do better. But Jeb was wily, and inevitably, we would slack off and he would be gone.

Being a bird dog, when he found something especially fragrant—a dead animal, for instance—he would roll in it. When he came home, he seemed almost eager to share his good fortune. Wanted everybody to smell what he had found. So he would try to get close and make contact. Whatever you were doing, you had to drop it and fill the galvanized wash tub we kept for this purpose with warm soapy water and give Jeb a bath. Afterwards, your hands carried the faint, sick smell of rotting flesh.

If he couldn't find something dead, then the manure pile at a nearby farm would serve as a tolerable substitute. Jeb preferred the newer, fresher manure, and I got used to hearing one of my daughters call out to me with the news, "Dad, Jeb's home and he's green again."

I would stop what I was doing and go fill the washtub. Afterwards, my hands smelled of cow flop.

Jeb hated these baths, by the way, and before you could wash him, you had to change into work clothes and, then, wash them and, sometimes bathe yourself. After a while, all of our good beach towels had become stained, smelly Jeb towels.

"Can't you *explain* things to him?" my wife said after she'd given a green Jeb his customary soapy bath.

"I don't know," I said. "I imagine he thinks he smells just lovely. Like a teenage boy drenched in bay rum."

He brought home other trophies. Parts of old carcasses—deer, usually—done in by the Vermont winter. There was something especially gruesome about the sight of a gnawed foreleg on the breezeway when you went out in the morning.

And, of course, on one of his rambles Jeb found a skunk. That, anyway, was the clear inference. Several warm, soapy baths and half a dozen quarts of tomato juice later, he still smelled.

"I may never be able to drink another Bloody Mary," my wife said.

Jeb seemed to know that we didn't want him to go outside unsupervised, and that we especially didn't want him off cruising the countryside, rolling in manure and aggravating the owners of female dogs in heat.

So in his mind, it became a game. They want me in; I want to be out. Let's see who wins.

If you were about to leave the house on an errand, Jeb would scoot out of the door ahead of you and stand in the driveway, looking back at you.

"Come on, Jeb," you'd say. "Back inside. Let's go."

He would take a few steps in your direction. Then stop. The gap between you wouldn't be that wide. No more than ten or fifteen feet. But as much as you would call and cajole, he wouldn't come any closer.

"Now come *on*, Jeb. I'm late. I have to go and you need to be inside."

No dice.

"Jeb, *here*."

Not buying it.

So you would think to yourself that if you moved quickly, you could catch him before he realized what you were doing.

Fat chance.

As soon as you made your move, Jeb would dance off another ten or fifteen feet and stand there, loose like a basketball player trying to keep you from driving to the bucket.

"Dammit, Jeb."

Come on. Try to get me. Show me your best move.

You'd make another rush and he would dance away again, maybe letting you get closer this time.

"Jeb, I'm going to *kill* you."

Maybe. But you've got to catch me first.

Another rush and you would be grabbing air.

This little game of keepaway would go on until you got tired, gave up, and went off on your errand with Jeb still standing in the yard, looking pleased with himself and ready to play. He never got tired of it.

Sometimes, he liked it so much he wouldn't quit, even when you were in the car, heading down the driveway, late and frustrated and out of breath.

"I swear," I said one night, "I thought about running him over. I was that mad. Made me feel terrible."

"Let it go," Marsha said. "You couldn't have hit him if you'd tried."

I'd assumed that things would get better as Jeb got older, but instead, they got worse. When spring came, I started trying to work with him in the yard. I decided to start all over, back where he was when he was just a little eight-week-old puppy, bold but biddable.

But it was, I soon decided, hopeless. When he was on a lead, Jeb was docile, and even cowed, which given his personality was both unusual and a little disconcerting. His tail would droop and so would his head, and he would look sort of woeful. Seeing him that way made me feel like I was being too heavy-handed, and I would go soft.

But, of course, when I released him, he would run off, out of control.

The thing wasn't working and it was my fault. I hadn't done the hard work and the follow-up after that initial training, with Hadley helping (and, actually, doing the best work). Now, I feared, it was too late. I had lost him.

So, I had to finally face a cold fact. Jeb was still young and unknowable, but I was not. I was, however poorly, the finished product, and I simply did not have the temperament to be a dog trainer. I lacked patience and could not detach myself and proceed by the numbers. Couldn't stick to the routine and couldn't keep my emotions out of it.

And, as the days got longer and longer, it became harder and harder to keep him around. I didn't want a kennel dog, even one that *could* hunt. And exiling Jeb to some wire cage at this point in his life, after he'd become part of the family—well, that was unthinkable.

So we endured more and more rambles and more and more soapy baths in the galvanized tub. More calls from irate neighbors. More worry about Jeb crossing a road on one of his jaunts and getting run down by a speeding pickup.

Much as we loved him, Jeb was becoming a bigger burden than I was willing to bear. I did a lot of tortured thinking about the whole situation and then, since he was my responsibility, took it upon myself to make a decision without consulting Marsha or the girls.

"Listen, are you interested in a young pointer?" I said one day in a phone conversation with my friend, Ted Hatfield, who was, at the time, living in St. Joseph, Missouri, where he owned a company that made black-powder rifles and side-by-side shotguns. I knew that he was a hunter, loved pointers, and at present was without a dog.

"You're not talking about Jeb?" he said, sounding surprised and a little disappointed in me. Ted is an optimist and doesn't recognize the existence of that thing people call "the downside."

"I just can't handle him, man," I said, and then poured out my heart.

Ted listened to my laments for a while and finally interrupted. "Hell, man, you can't get rid of Jeb. You love the old dog and he loves you. Besides, he was a present. You can't do that to yourself or your girls."

I felt properly ashamed of myself, but persisted. "You don't understand . . ."

"Give me a break," Ted said. "He just sounds like a normal two-year-old pointer to me. And not as bad as some I know."

"Well, I guess I'm just not a pointer man, then. Not tough enough."

"Bullshit. Listen, I'll make you a deal. I know a fellow out here who trains dogs. I believe he can turn the sorriest specimen on legs into a passable hunting dog if you give him the time. I'll talk to him and see if he can make room in his schedule for Jeb. If he can, you call him and set it up. Then, after he's worked with Jeb for a while, and you've seen the results, if you still want to get rid of him, then I'll take him."

The clear implication was that he would also think less of me.

"Okay," I said. "Sounds like a plan."

"I'll get back to you. Trust me, you and I will be shooting pointed quail over that dog next season."

"*Right.*"

"You gotta believe, man."

"All right, Reverend," I said. "I believe. But I've still got to see it."

ELEVEN

A couple of days later, I had my first phone conversation with John Hann, who ran an operation he called "Perfection Kennels," which sounded awfully ambitious to me. At this point, I would have settled for "Pretty Good Kennels," or even "So-So Kennels."

"So I talked to Ted," John said. He spoke slowly and softly and almost without inflection. It was the kind of voice that, if he'd been your doctor, would have comforted you during a tough diagnosis.

"Then he told you about my problem?"

"Not much. He just said you had a dog that needed some training. Tell me about him."

So I recited the same litany I'd given to Ted, trying to keep the self-pity out of my voice this time.

John listened without interrupting, and it was almost as though I was talking to myself. When I finished, he said, "I see."

"Does it sound like something you can fix?" I said, expecting him to say, more or less, that it was past hope.

"Oh sure. I mean, I won't know what kind of dog he'll be in the field until I've had a chance to work with him. I'll need to see what kind of nose he has and how he responds to birds. But we'll get him under control."

He made it sound like there was nothing to it, and I vaguely resented his confidence. *Oh, yeah*, I thought, *well, you haven't seen Jeb yet. This might be one nut even* you *can't crack.*

But what I said was, "That would be a real gift to me and my girls."

Hann didn't seem to think that was worth any comment. He merely said, "Well, let's get him out here and see what we've got."

The way it worked out, I had to make a trip to Australia, so we lined up airline transportation to Kansas City for Jeb the same day I flew from Hartford, Connecticut, to Los Angeles, and then, on to Sydney. I loaded Jeb's traveling crate in the bed of my pickup and put him in the front seat with me, early in the morning, before dawn. He was excited. Probably thought we were going hunting even though it wasn't the season and I was wearing a sport coat. When we got to the airport and I put him in the crate, he started howling.

"He ever done this before?" the man at the loading dock asked while he did the paperwork.

"No. First time."

"Well, if he keeps that up, the passengers will hear him all the way to KayCee."

"He'll settle down," I said, hopefully.

When the paperwork was done, I looked at Jeb through the wire mesh of the crate and said, "I'll see you in a couple of months, bud. You be a good dog."

He howled even louder and more pitifully, and the sound of Jeb in distress seemed to ring in my ears, all the way across the Pacific.

A couple of weeks later, I came home to an adoring welcome home from my wife and daughters. As soon as it was polite, I asked Marsha if there had been any news about Jeb.

"No," she said. "Nothing."

"Well," I said, "I guess that means he got there, at least. Somebody would have called if there had been a problem, right?"

"Sure. Don't worry. I'm sure Jeb is fine."

It was too late to call that night, but in the morning, I went to my office and checked my answering machine.

There was nothing from John Hann, but there were a number of business calls, a few of which were even important. I called Hann before I made any of them.

"How was your trip?" John asked.

"Fine," I said, impatiently. "Great country. How's Jeb?"

"Oh, he's fine."

Nothing more. Just fine.

"You're working with him, then?"

"Oh sure. Every day."

"And how," I asked, dreading the answer, "is he doing?"

"Jeb is a good dog," John said mildly, which was the only way he said anything, and I felt like I'd been told my kid was adjusting well at camp. Fitting in with all the other kids and enjoying himself.

I felt, in short, this immense sense of relief and then, immediately, I wanted to know if my kid was beating out the other campers in any competitions. Would he be bringing home any blue ribbons.

"Will he be a hunting dog, then?" I asked, hopefully.

"Jeb has a good nose. I wouldn't call it a great nose, but he'll make a bird dog for sure."

It was all I needed to hear but, of course, I wanted to hear more. I tried to tease some details out of John but he isn't one for long phone conversations. He did say that he'd had to "correct" some bad habits and help Jeb "unlearn" a few things, but that it hadn't been much of a problem and he expected Jeb to make good progress.

"Will you be coming out to pick him up yourself?"

"Yes."

"That's good. You should plan on staying a couple of days. Then I can work some with you, too."

That was how he liked to work, he explained. Owners needed training, too.

I certainly couldn't argue with that, I said, and we settled on some dates about six weeks off.

I hung up the phone feeling happy, and then skeptical. I'd have to see it. And probably then, I still wouldn't believe it.

I stayed with Ted Hatfield in Missouri. I got in too late to visit Hann, but I was up early the next morning and I followed his directions until I came to the kennel. He hadn't even started working with the dogs when I got there.

"Looking to get an early start?" he said after we'd shaken hands. He seemed amused by my eagerness.

"I suppose so," I said.

"You want some coffee," he asked, "or would you like to get right to it?"

He was a tall man with good, strong features. He moved as deliberately as he talked and there was a kind of ineffable gentleness about him, so you couldn't imagine him ever rushing things, getting distracted, or losing his temper. I felt confident about him five minutes after meeting him.

I passed on the coffee and followed him out behind his house to the kennels, which held about a dozen dogs, most of them pointers. They all came to the front of their runs when they saw Hann and began barking and pawing at the wire, asking to be let out. I took that as a good sign. His training methods couldn't be too hard-nosed, I thought, if all these dogs were begging him for some more of it.

Jeb was in a run at the far end of the kennel and he was demonstrating just like the other dogs. He looked fine. Maybe a little thinner, but, then, he probably wasn't cadging any table scraps out here.

I'd wondered if Jeb would recognize me. Had we bonded enough so that he would miss me and be glad to see me and all that? It was rank sentimentalism, but, anyone who doesn't get emotional about his dog has to be a hard case.

When Hann opened the door to Jeb's run, he came right to me and jumped up so his feet were on my chest. He was wagging his tail fiercely and his mouth was open in what I interpreted to be a smile.

If he was happy to see me, then I imagine I was even happier to see him. I had missed him.

"Hey, bud," I said, rubbing his ears. "How you doing? Good to see you, man. You been a good boy?"

This went on for a minute or two before John Hann, who was standing ten or fifteen feet behind me, spoke. His voice was soft, but firm. "Okay, Jeb. Here."

Jeb dropped down on all four feet, moved over next to Hann's right leg, and stood there as immobile as a soldier on parade. After a couple of seconds, Hann reached down and gave Jeb a tap on his flank.

"Okay, Jeb," he said

Jeb moved out, at a sort of easy lope, in the direction where Hann was looking. When he'd gone twenty yards or so, Hann said, with the same tone of authority. "Whoa."

Jeb stopped cold in his tracks.

"*Jeb?*" I said, skeptically, not quite believing this was the same dog.

"Okay, now," Hann said, "walk up to him and tap him on top of the head, lightly, to release him."

Jeb did not move a muscle as I approached and remained staunch right up until the moment I tapped him on the head. Then, paying no attention to me, he started moving again. He was working for the man and, right now, the man was John Hann.

I stood there and marveled while Hann put Jeb through his paces. When Hann said, "Whoa," Jeb locked up like a statue and did not move—not one paw—until he was released by a tap on the head. When Hann said, "Here," Jeb turned, ran straight to him, and stood motionless at his right leg. When Jeb was on the run and his name was called, he would change direction—turning right or left ninety degrees—and keep moving on that line until he was either called or had gone about forty yards; then, he would turn back in the other direction, perfectly coursing the ground in front of him.

"It's a miracle," I said. "I truly cannot believe it. How did you do it?"

"Just takes time. You work with them every day and, little by little, they get it."

Easy for you to say, I thought, and said, "Well, all I can say is you are a genius. I'd have never believed it."

I spent a large part of two days with Hann, and during that time, he taught me how to work with Jeb. Mastering the commands was easy enough. In fact, I already knew the three essentials: When I wanted the dog to come to me, I said "Here." That meant he was to come in, right now, to my side and stand there until I released him with a soft slap to his flank. When I said, "Whoa," he was to freeze, right where he was, and remain there, unmoving, until I came up and tapped him on the head to release him. And when he was running out ahead of me and heard his name, he was to change direction, left or right, by about ninety degrees.

"Fetch" and "stay" and "kennel up" could be mixed in along with anything else that seemed to work. But those first three, Hann explained, were the essentials. With them, I could control him in the field.

"And that's what you want. The dog has to be under your control. He'll learn about the birds with experience. I've done a fair amount with him, using release birds, and there is a covey in the field over there that he's pointed a time or two. So he knows his way around birds, and the more time he spends in the field, hunting, the better he'll get. But it's wasted time if the dog isn't under control."

That much I already knew. Only too well.

Most of the time I spent with Hann was devoted to using the shock collar, which he'd used to train Jeb and told me I would need to keep using.

Not just for the short term, either. "You may never stop using one," Hann said. "And that's all right. It is the best way yet to control and to make sure he knows you are in control."

The shock collar—known euphemistically as a "remote trainer"—is a simple device, consisting of a transmitter that sends a signal to a set of electrical leads on a dog collar. The leads are in contact with the dog's neck, and the transmitter's signal sends a small, battery-powered charge through them. When this happens, the dog gets an electrical shock. The shock can be weak, moderate, or strong depending on a setting determined by the operator, which, ideally, would be severe enough to get the dog's attention but not hurt him.

The shock collar has been around for twenty years or more, and when it first came along, it was thought to be capable of working miracles. Now, when a dog was disobeying or ignoring his handler or master, it was not necessary to chase him down and catch him before you could "correct" him (or punish him, if you prefer). This solved one of the great paradoxes of dog training. When a dog makes a mistake, it is important to correct him and scold him and even whip him, right then, so he associates the punishment with the act. But if the dog is out of handling range, what can you do other than yell and scream and stomp your feet? And, if you call the dog and he comes in, you certainly can't scold or whip him then. Do that and the dog will figure that coming when called is a mug's game. All it gets you is a ration of grief.

So, before the shock collar came along, the ideal was this: If your dog made a mistake or disobeyed, you caught him, took him back to the scene of the crime, and started over again with stern words and firm hands. The ideal and the reality were often separated by a wide breach.

Then came the shock collar, and now if, for instance, your dog didn't come when you called him or stop when you commanded "Whoa," you did not have to chase him down, catch him, and go through the drill all over again. You could touch a button and "remind" him of what he was supposed to be doing . . . or not doing, as the case might be.

However, as we all know, miraculous technological breakthroughs come complete with a downside. Cell phones are marvelous when you need one and a colossal nuisance when some young thing is sitting next to you in the airport, talking loudly into one about her boyfriend. Shock collars were fine in the right hands. In the wrong—often ignorant—hands, they could brutalize a dog and make him afraid to hunt.

I'd learned this, a few years before I met John Hann, when I heard a man who knew something about dogs refer to a certain English setter as "a blinker."

"What's that?" I asked.

"A blinker is a dog that, when he smells birds, he doesn't point and he doesn't rush in and scatter them. What he does is kind of blink and then tiptoe on around those birds, without letting on he knows they're there. The only sign is that little blink. And you have to know how to look for it."

"What causes it?" I said.

"Shock collars," the man said. "No. Correct that. Damn fools who misuse shock collars. What happens is this: Fellow gets a young, untrained dog and figures the shock collar is his magic wand. He can just point it at the dog, mash down on the button, and *presto* . . . instead of a mutt, he's got him a wizard. But the shock collar doesn't excuse you from doing the hard work of dog training. Or from thinking, either.

"What a shock collar does provide is negative reinforcement. Do something wrong and you get a jolt. Just to remind you. If you do right, pay your taxes, and go to church every Sunday, then no shock. The collar can't give an ordinary dog a great nose, and it sure can't make everything come out right in the field.

"But you'll see these fellows. They've got the young dog and the brand-new shock collar and they want championship performance. The dog crowds some birds and they flush. Common mistake, and most dogs eventually learn on their own that they've got to hold back. But the man with the collar, he's impatient. So when the dog crowds birds and they flush, he zaps the dog. And he usually has the juice turned up because he wants to be sure the dog gets the message. Sometimes, that shock will be enough to roll a dog.

"Well, after a few times crowding birds and getting shocked, the dog figures it out this way: 'If I get into birds, generally I get fried; but as long as I'm just loping along, not putting up any birds or pointing any birds, everything is fine. So what I'll do is this—if I smell birds, I will detour smartly around them and not let on.'

"Of course, when he first smells the birds, the dog blinks. It's a reflex. He can't help it. And that's why you call 'em 'blinkers.'"

"And you've actually seen dogs like this?" I asked.

"Lots of them."

"I'll be damned."

"These dogs ain't stupid. I'd say if anyone was stupid, it's the fellow with the transmitter in his hand. Stupid, and sometimes outright cruel and sadistic. You see them, loud and angry, using the collar to get even with the dog. That kind generally don't even like dogs, and maybe not even bird hunting. They're just doing it for the same reason that some men play golf—because they think they have to. They're just interested in the score, and when they can't kill birds, they get mad at the dog. They're mad at a lot of things, actually, and they use the shock collar to work off some of that anger.

"Yessir, I would say that the shock collar has helped—notice I said *helped*, not *made*—a lot of fine bird dogs. But it's ruined a fair number, too."

After I heard that story, I had decided against using a collar on my first dog, Molly. She was small and fairly delicate, and I didn't want to dampen her spirits. And, truth was, I'd gotten her as a trained dog and never really needed to make a lot of corrections.

"Well, you'll need to make them with Jeb," John Hann said when I told him this. "He is young. He's a male. And he's a pointer. That's three for three. You'll need the collar, for sure. So you might as well learn to use it right."

So we went to work.

The first step was to get me used to the idea of the shock collar. "I suspect you'll be a little nervous about using it on your dog. Even when you're mad at him, you don't really want to hurt him. And a lot of people think using electricity to shock a dog is cruel."

I nodded. I didn't think of myself as a softie when it came to dogs, but I admit, I did have some qualms about the collar. So detached and so . . . *remote*, turning the euphemism on its head.

"Here," Hann said, handing me the collar.

I took it.

"Now, here's the transmitter. Put your fingers on the leads and try it. See how much it hurts."

I wrapped my fingers around the two bald electrical leads and with some trepidation (I had to do it, Hann was watching me), touched the transmitter. My fingers leapt back from the leads. The current was noticeable, and the best description of the sensation might be to say that it "stung." But it certainly didn't hurt, and it didn't traumatize me. I'd had worse shocks testing a car engine to see if there was a spark.

"Now, that's not really going to hurt Jeb or turn him into a mental case, right?"

"I seriously doubt it."

"And you just give him a little shot. You don't clamp down on it. You just want him to feel it and be reminded."

"Okay."

(I should say here that when I got home and got my very own shock collar, I tried the test with it turned up to the highest setting. I wrapped my hand around the collar, to get a grip, and put two fingers on the leads. When I touched the transmitter, the collar flew out of my hands and I sat down, involuntarily, in my chair. It was a serious jolt.

The only reason I can imagine for using the collar at that setting is for aversion training that will keep your dog alive. To break him of running cars or deer, for example. Or to make sure he knows not to get close to snakes.)

Hann put the collar on Jeb now, and we went out for a walk. I put Jeb through the usual series of commands and he responded flawlessly. I wondered if I'd actually even need to use the collar.

"What's going to happen," Hann said, "is that he's going to get to hunting and he's going to forget that he's got that thing on. And then, he's going to forget that he's supposed to be doing this with you. He'll start to go off on his own and that's when you'll have to correct him."

After about fifteen minutes in the field next to John's house, Jeb did, indeed, lose concentration and fall into his old habit of running out ahead for the sheer exuberant hell of it.

"Call him."

I shouted, "*Here.*"

Jeb did not turn and immediately begin coming my way.

"Okay. Reach out and touch him."

I pressed the transmitter button. Jeb flinched and immediately turned.

"Now call him again."

Jeb came straight to me and stood resolutely at my side until I slapped his flank to release him.

"See what I mean," Hann said. "It's sort of a strong reminder."

I learned, gradually, to be comfortable using the shock collar. I learned how not to be either too quick on the trigger or too reluctant to hit the transmitter when Jeb didn't respond to one of my commands. And, I got used to the idea that the shock was not really hurting my dog and that if you used the collar properly, you didn't have to use it very often. After a "correction," Jeb would behave like a model citizen for what seemed like a long time . . . especially according to *his* time horizons, which were exceedingly short.

The collar, in fact, made life easier for both of us, and it certainly didn't seem to cut down on his pleasure at being in the field. He moved with his customary exuberance, running out ahead like simple movement was the absolute greatest joy in life. The difference was, he now stayed within sight of me. In fact, he had learned to check back on his own if he thought he was getting out too far. I seldom had to call him in closer, and we moved through the knee-high grass in the field next to Hann's house in a kind of purposeful silence. Jeb did his work and I watched. Which is how it is supposed to be. This, paradoxically, is the source of bird hunting's deep satisfaction. You are not *really* the hunter in this exercise. But you do get to admire a real hunter at work.

Toward evening on my second day under John Hann's tutelage, we were walking along an old, overgrown fence line in the field next to his house. Jeb was up ahead, at the proper range, coursing the field like an old pro. Hann and I were talking about this and that, and I had taken my eye off Jeb.

Then, Hann said, "Look at that."

I looked up ahead and Jeb was on a point, and to my biased eyes, it looked like a very stylish point. His tail was high and just a little crooked—he would never be able to entirely straighten that tail and I looked on that as the handicap he had nobly overcome, though he certainly wasn't aware of anything like that. Anyway . . . his tail was high, the way a dog on point should hold it, and his neck was thrust out so his head was like the tip of a spear, pointing directly at a target. He was stock-still; a picture of pure purpose.

"There is a covey of quail that uses this field. I believe that's what he's got pointed. Go on up and flush them."

I walked up on Jeb and could see he was quivering, just slightly, with anticipation.

"Good man," I said, and walked on past him in the direction he was pointing.

The birds startled me when they came out of the grass, and I am sure that I had never been so thrilled with a covey flush since my first one.

My dog, I thought. *How good is that?*

As soon as I had recovered my composure, I looked back at Jeb to see how he had reacted. He was still standing on point and, as far as I could tell, hadn't moved a muscle.

"Tap him to release him."

I did. Then I wanted to tell him "Good dog," and rub his ears, but he didn't have time for any of that. He was moving again, off after the singles.

I wondered if Hann had somehow arranged for that covey to be there. To show off his work in the most undeniable way.

"No," he said. "You don't ever know where they'll be."

"Well, it was a helluva show."

"He did all right," Hann said. "I think you'll have a better bird season with him this year."

"John," I said, "I was thinking about not even hunting this year. Now, I can't wait."

"Well, that's good. I'm glad to hear it."

"I can't thank you enough."

TWELVE

When I got home, bird season was still almost two months off. I was eager but there wasn't anything for it. Time, as they say, takes its time.

But, if I couldn't hunt with Jeb, I could still take him out and work him. And I liked doing this, especially if I had an audience. After they'd seen Jeb do "Whoa" about a hundred times, my wife and daughters got tired of our act. But there were still my bird-hunting buddies and other friends who I would invite over for a beer in the evening.

I'd tell them about this great trainer I'd found—being careful to give the real credit to Ted Hatfield—and how he had worked miracles with my dog. Then I'd bring Jeb out so he could show them his stuff. They were invariably impressed. Or said so, anyway. And one of them asked me for Hann's number so he could call him about training his own dog, which he described as "a setter of pretty good breeding but no manners at all."

These little backyard demonstrations were just a childish way of showing off, and after a while, even I realized it. They were brief sessions, too short to really keep Jeb sharp. So after a couple of weeks, I knocked that stuff off and started taking him to a large open area about five miles from the house. I didn't want to take him to an actual bird cover for the good reason that it was against the law to train a dog on wild birds out of season. Also, I figured that when Jeb started pointing birds, I wanted to be there with the gun. Otherwise, he might forget we were a team and I'd have to send him to Missouri for a refresher course.

The field where I worked him was ideal. Big enough so that he could run, and flat enough so that I could keep him in sight. We started going there late in the afternoon every day.

Once I'd parked, Jeb would pile out of the truck and sit with his neck extended to make it easier for me to put the shock collar on him. He seemed to think this was just an inevitable component of the drill; nothing optional about it.

Once the collar was on, he would stand up and wait for me to release him, which I would do by slapping him on the flank and saying, "Okay, Jeb. Hunt 'em up."

And he would take off, to begin coursing the field with me walking behind him, watching like a parent proud of a kid who has just learned how to ride a bicycle.

I'd give the "Whoa" command and he would stop. Call "Here," and he would come to me. Shout his name and he would change direction. All the commands that Hann had taught him, and he obeyed them instantly. I seldom had to use the collar.

We both enjoyed these sessions and this, to say the least, was something different. I looked forward eagerly to getting out at the end of the day and working harmoniously with my dog, but not, by a long shot, as eagerly as Jeb did. When it got to be late afternoon and he saw me putting on my boots and picking up the little canvas bag that held the shock collar and other training tools, he'd react with something like a frenzy. He would start barking and charging around the house and turning around in circles. In doing this, he would manage to ball up all the throw rugs in the house. I had to start putting my boots on in the breezeway, in secret, before I called to him from out there. This way, by the time he caught on to the plan, he was outside where his antics couldn't do anything worse than scratch out a patch or two of grass.

Pleasant—almost languidly so—as these sessions were, I did learn something from them. For one thing, I discovered that my dog definitely had the pointer gene for stoicism.

One afternoon, we went a little farther up in the field than usual and were working along a border of tall trees. Jeb was running ahead of me, not quite flat out, but certainly as fast as I'd want to see him move in bird cover. Then, suddenly, he recoiled almost as though he had run into a glass wall. He paused and stood still for a moment. Then, he shook his head as though trying to clear it after he'd taken a hard blow.

I couldn't see anything that would have stopped him like that and, foolishly, went on with the walk. Jeb didn't act as though there was anything wrong, and for another ten or fifteen minutes we kept moving along through the field. He was doing such a good job, and enjoying himself so much, that I didn't whoa him or call him in, merely shouted his name now and then so he would change direction.

Finally, I decided it was time to get home for dinner, so I called to him.

"Here," I shouted and Jeb turned and headed for me, running so hard his ears were pinned back. He was clearly not out of gas.

When he was standing next to me I got down on one knee to rub his ears and give him a little show of appreciation. That's when I saw a long gash in his brisket with the skin hanging off it in strips that were at least an inch long. The cut was deep and clean and because of where it was, there wasn't much blood. I could see bone.

"Oh, buddy. What did you do?"

He didn't seem to be in pain and he certainly didn't want to quit running. So I released him and let him run ahead, and when we went by the place where he'd stopped so abruptly, I investigated and found what I now suspected: a strand of old, rusted barbed wire, strung taut between two of the large trees. I looked more closely and found the barb that had peeled open the skin over Jeb's chest. There were tufts of his hair caught on it.

Jeb never stopped running, all the way back to the truck, and to look at him from a distance, you wouldn't have known he was injured. I left him in the truck when I got to the house, went inside, and called the vet. It was after office hours and she was at home. In the years to come, she would get used to getting calls from me at odd hours. She told me to bring him on out and didn't seem to mind. Jean Ceglowski is an animal lover and a good and cheerful neighbor. She and her husband, both Cornell grads, share a practice in Rupert, Vermont, which is some twelve miles from my house on a route I could now drive with my eyes closed. Her husband's name is Eugene, so it's Gene and Jean; when you call and ask for "Jean," and the receptionist does not recognize your voice, she asks, "Which one?"

Jean met Jeb and me at the door.

"He looks good," she said. "You must be working him a lot."

"I am. And he's doing great. Except for the occasional run-in with some old barbed wire."

"Well, let's put him up on the table and have a look."

I lifted Jeb up on the cold, stainless-steel examining table, and for the first time, he started to shiver. This usually meant shots, and who needs that?

"That is a nasty one," Jean said. But her tone was calm. She'd seen much worse.

"Funny thing is," I said, "he doesn't seem to mind. Doesn't even seem to notice."

"Well, it's not a particularly sensitive area. And he's a tough guy, aren't you, Jeb?"

Jeb wagged his tail tepidly, like he knew the sweet talk was a con. The prelude, no doubt, to something unpleasant, like a rabies shot.

"We need to close that up. I don't have anyone here with me; do you mind holding him?"

"No," I said. "Of course not."

So I held Jeb, who was still trembling a little, while Jean washed out the gash and disinfected it. Jeb didn't make a sound and actually stopped trembling, almost as though he was relieved. If this was her best shot, he could take it.

When the wound was clean, Jean pulled the flaps of skin together and instead of using needle and thread, she stapled them together, without using any anesthetic. When she finished, there were four shiny wires in Jeb's hide. He never flinched or whimpered during the whole process.

"He's a stout one," Jean said.

"Comes with the breed," I said.

"That's true."

We made a little small talk, and she gave me some pills and the instructions for administering them. I asked her if she'd seen any birds on the horseback rides she takes through some good grouse country on a ridge beyond her house.

"Quite a few, actually."

"Well, you'll probably run into us up there once the season starts."

I took Jeb home and gave him a treat for dinner—a little bacon grease on top of his dry food. I expected him to stiffen up and to show some sign of pain and distress that night, but those staples might have been spray-painted on for all the awareness he showed of them. I was going to give him the next day off, but he didn't seem to want that, and I figured I wouldn't be doing him any favors by keeping him inside. So we went through our evening devotionals, just like we always did, and he ran like it was pure bliss (although we did stay away from the corner of the field where the barbed wire was strung).

But, as I found out—time and again—you cannot protect a hard-going bird dog from all the hazards of this world. There are too many of them, and, anyway, even if there were only one, a dog like Jeb would find it and get into it. There were more trips to Jean's for repairs. Many of them.

THIRTEEN

Bird season came around at last. Jeb and I went out opening day and, while my expectations were high, the (tiny) rational portion of my brain knew that they were unrealistic. He was still a young dog and so far, all his progress had been made under classroom conditions. Now, we were going out into the unforgiving field.

But he found birds and pointed them, and if I had performed as well as he, then we would have brought home something for the table. While he had been practicing, however, I had not fired a shotgun for nine months. I missed one easy shot on a grouse that Jeb pointed like an old pro.

"Sorry, bud. I let you down," I said, and meant every word.

He pointed two other birds that got up in range, but the foliage was so thick that by the time I got the gun mounted, they were nothing to me but the sound of furiously beating wings.

"My bad."

Jeb gave me a look, as though to say, "Hey, man. What *about* it?"

Still, while we came home empty-handed, I told Marsha that I couldn't remember a better opening day.

"Well, when it cools off a little, and the leaves are down, I want to go out with you and see this miracle dog in action."

"I can't wait for you to go."

I was proud like the parent of the kid who has the lead in the school play—and probably just as insufferable. And I can't say exactly why. What did I, after all, have to be proud of? The dog had the talent and John Hann had shaped it and molded it, like an expert director. I was just the backer, living on borrowed glory.

But willing to take it and unable to get enough.

Jeb and I went out every day. Late one afternoon in the middle of the first week of the season, when we were up on the ridge behind Jean Ceglowski's office (he'd started trembling when we drove past it), Jeb hit a point on the edge of an old, gone-by apple orchard. The point was firm and the place was right, and I figured there had to be a bird there. I made sure of my approach and walked in briskly so the bird would be forced to fly, instead of running. Jeb was quivering, I noticed, when I went by him.

The grouse got up, making more noise than seemed possible, but I got the gun up cleanly to my shoulder. It was an easy, going-away shot, and when I touched the trigger the bird dropped decisively. The shot seemed to echo for a long time and a couple of feathers hung in the air where the bird had been.

I looked back and Jeb was holding his ground, still on point.

I walked to him and touched him on the head.

"Okay, Jeb," I said. "Hunt dead."

He broke from the point and ran to the spot where the bird had fallen. He nosed around eagerly in the grass, then stopped. When he raised his head, he was holding the bird in his mouth, looking triumphant.

"Good man. Fetch him here."

He pranced all the way in; prouder of his performance, even, than I was.

I admired the bird. The wonderful mix of browns and blacks on the feathers that covered the sturdy, compact body. Like any hunter, I felt a kind of melancholy satisfaction. Even when it is only a bird, and one with barely a 10 percent chance of surviving the winter, at this moment you appreciate the poignancy of José Ortega y Gasset's famous formulation: *One does not hunt in order to kill; on the contrary, one kills in order to have hunted.*

Jeb was not into this kind of deep-think, ponderous bullshit. He wanted to find more birds. And he did. I didn't get the shots, though. Too much leaf cover.

But it didn't make any difference. The day—maybe even the season—could have ended with that first bird and I would have been content. This was the way the thing was meant to be. And when it is that way, it is sublime.

Marsha and I ate that bird for dinner. Cooked in a 350-degree oven with some bacon strips over the breast to keep it moist. The flesh was white and tender with a flavor that was both subtle and wild, suggestive of the things that grouse eat—apples, grapes, nuts, wintergreen. A taste that cannot be captured or domesticated, or even, for that matter, described. We served the bird with wild rice and acorn squash and a bottle of what we thought of as a good red wine. Something, probably, from Chile or Argentina, with flavor that exceeded its pedigree.

It was a fitting dinner; a proper celebration.

"Now," Marsha said, toward the end of the meal, "I *really* want to go out with you two."

That day came, about two weeks later, and by then I was starting to think of us—Jeb and me, that is—as a well-oiled bird-finding and killing (sometimes) machine. And, in truth, we were having some success. There were a lot of birds in Vermont that year. In my experience, the famous population swings are not as pronounced in New England as they are in the Great Lakes states, but there is a definite cycle, and that year, we were near its peak. Jeb was finding a lot of birds and I was shooting some of them.

So when I took Marsha out on a bright, brisk October Sunday, I had visions. Jeb would point half a dozen birds or more, and Marsha would get some open shots and put a bird or two in the bag. We would come home and brush Jeb out in front of the fire and then have another candlelight dinner with a bottle of that good Chilean red. What could be better?

And things started out all right. Jeb made a couple of points, but it was a windy day and the birds were a little skittish and flushed out of range. Still, Marsha got to see Jeb work and was impressed.

"I can't believe he is the same dog," she said.

"He isn't. He has been reborn."

We hit a barren stretch and I suggested another covert. On the way there, we stopped at a little country store—the kind you find in every New England town—and bought a jug of local apple cider and a wedge of Vermont cheddar. We ate the cheese and drank the cider while we sat on a crumbling old stone wall near where I parked the truck.

"Can you imagine the work . . . no, the *labor*," I said, contemplating the wall.

One of the cerebral pleasures of hunting birds in Vermont is studying the landscape for signs of its history. In that portion of the state where we live, virtually all of the ground, except the very tops of the high mountains, was once cleared for farming. The hardy souls who did this took the rocks turned up by their plows and laid them methodically, two on one, to make stone walls. You'll find them a mile back in from the nearest road, on ground that is now grown up in mature second-growth hardwoods, and you cannot help but feel a kind of awe for the sheer, back-breaking work that it took to make those walls, and a kind of wistfulness for the way people's ambitions and works are worn down by time.

"Where do you suppose the kids and grandkids are now?"

"California, probably. And glad to be out of farming."

Jeb stayed in the bed of the truck while we had our little picnic. He whined impatiently and when I let him out, he took off in a hurry, like he had to make up for lost time.

"Don't you think you ought to bring him in?" Marsha said. "He's awfully wide."

"He does that," I said, smugly, "when I first let him out. He'll check back in."

"What if he doesn't?"

"I've got the shock collar," I said. "And what's more important is, he knows it."

"I see."

We had gone about two hundred yards on the line Jeb took when we heard him. He was howling, and it was the sound of a dog on some kind of scent and making chase. I didn't know what it was but I didn't like it.

"Here," I shouted as loud as I could. I thought he might be running a deer and had my finger on the transmitter button, ready to shock him, when the sound changed in quality. It became more high-pitched and was now, clearly, a cry of distress.

"Oh, man," I said, and ran toward the sound. I imagined Jeb tangled in wire or standing down a coyote or bear. Something bad.

I met him coming my way and from the way he was running, I could tell he was in pain. His tail was between his legs and his head was down and he was moving erratically.

"Here," I shouted, and he came straight to me, like he wanted me to protect him. Something about his face didn't look right.

"What is it?" Marsha said, behind me.

"I don't know."

Then, I did. Jeb looked like he had grown a beard.

"Oh, Lord," I said. "He's gotten into a porcupine."

When he reached my side, I could see the quills sticking out of his muzzle at crazy angles. At least three dozen of them. One of them was stuck in his nose. Blood came from this wound and ran down his brisket. It hurt just to look at it.

I unloaded my gun and put it on the ground and put my hands on Jeb to steady him.

"Easy, buddy," I said. "Easy. We'll take care of it."

He started pawing at his face, trying to get the quills out, or at least, to get some relief from the pain.

"Easy. Easy. Take it easy."

He was a little short of frantic.

Marsha had reached us and when she looked at Jeb, she said, "Poor guy. Take it easy, buddy."

She stroked his flank and then said to me, "What do we do?"

"Well, let's get him home first. You take the guns and go get the truck, bring it up that old logging road as far as you can. I'll carry him and meet you."

She left with the guns and I picked Jeb up in my arms and followed.

He whimpered a little when I lifted him, but he seemed to realize that things would go better if he didn't fight it, so he stopped squirming. I staggered down the logging road, with Jeb in my arms, bleeding on my vest and shirt, until I met Marsha with the truck.

"We'll ride in the back," I said.

I put Jeb in the bed, then climbed in and sat next to him. He wanted to put his head in my lap, but when he tried it, that drove a couple of the quills in deeper and he flinched. We rode back to the house, with Jeb sitting in my lap and me rubbing his flanks and telling him that it would be all right.

But I wondered if it would. A couple of years earlier, a dog that belonged to a friend of mine had gotten into a porcupine, and one of the quills had gone up into the soft palate and, from there, into the brain. The dog had died from the injury. Jeb's jaws were firmly closed so I couldn't see how many quills were in there, and possibly stuck into the roof of his mouth. But from what I could see, he'd gotten the full treatment. As many quills as there were on the outside, I thought, there had to be some inside, too.

When we got home, Jeb and I waited in the truck while Marsha tried Jean and got her answering machine. On a nice afternoon like this, I guessed, she would be out riding.

"Now what?" Marsha said.

"Well, let's see what we can do. Get the needle-nosed pliers out of my tool bag. And wrap some ice cubes in a towel."

I remembered listening to another hunter telling a story about how he'd had to remove porcupine quills from his dog, and those tools seemed to be part of it. He'd also said something about using wire cutters on the quills. They were hollow, he'd explained, and cutting them allowed the air inside to escape. The deflated quills were easier to pull.

Still, I was winging it.

"Better bring some work gloves, too," I said.

When we had gathered all this, Marsha held Jeb by his collar and I clipped the first quill, then gripped it with the pliers and pulled. It came out easily enough, with a little spurt of blood. Jeb barely flinched.

"Good man," I said. "Just take it easy."

Some quills came easy and some, not so easy. After I'd pulled one, I would put the cold towel over the spot to numb it and blot up the blood. Jeb took it with surprising calmness, even when I pulled the one that was stuck in his nose.

"Lord," Marsha said, "that one hurt *me*."

"Okay," I said, when we'd gotten all the quills I could see. "That's the easy part. Now, you'd better put two hands on him while I go inside."

She gripped his collar tightly and I used my gloved left hand to pry open his mouth.

"Oh boy."

There were at least ten quills in there. One had gone all the way through his upper gum. A couple were in his tongue. I looked hard but couldn't see any stuck into the roof of his mouth.

"That's a relief," I said.

I started with the quills that looked like they were the least painful, realizing that this had to be a relative thing. I couldn't imagine sitting still with a knitting needle jammed into my tongue or lip.

I pulled the first one and Jeb strained, just slightly, at Marsha's grip. My hand was inside his mouth, with some very serious canine teeth an inch or two from my fingers. If he'd wanted to bite, just from reflex, there was no way I could stop him.

"My name might be 'Nubby' tomorrow."

"Please be careful."

"Rest assured."

I tried to pull firmly without jerking, and after each quill came out, I dabbed the spot with the cold towel. There was blood and saliva and ice water everywhere. I had to stop and clean things up so I could see what I was doing.

"Down to the two ugly ones."

"Are you sure you want to do this?"

"He's been good so far."

"He is a tough guy, I'll give him that. Stupid about porcupines, for sure, but plenty tough."

"All right. Let's go for it."

The quill that was stuck through Jeb's upper gum might have been an old nail, driven deep into a piece of hard oak. I had to pull hard just to get it to move. And it took three tries before it finally came out in a gush of blood.

"Reminds me of getting my wisdom teeth pulled," I said.

"I can't believe he let you do it. I can't take much more of this, myself."

"Last one."

There was no way, I decided, that I could remove that quill from Jeb's tongue without it hurting him. Maybe more than he could stand. I looked down at him and tightened my grip on his lower jaw.

"Okay, buddy," I said, trying to make my voice soothing. "This is the last one. You can handle it, right?"

And bless me if he didn't wag his tail. I'd have done anything for him, just then, and it seemed like the best thing I could do was get that quill out quick and clean. I clamped the pliers over it and squeezed down as hard as I could. Then I snatched my hand back, smooth and quick, trying to make the quill come out on the same line it went in. It came out with a spurt of blood and Jeb did not fight me or try to take my hand off.

"There," I said. "All done."

I wiped his muzzle with the cold towel and he wagged his tail and otherwise acted like he really appreciated my help.

"That was a hell of a show," Marsha said. I felt like I had run ten miles.

We cleaned up the mess, then made a bed for Jeb in front of the woodstove, assuming he'd want to sleep off the trauma. But he wouldn't lie down. We thought, at first, that the pain might be too much for him and we gave him a couple of aspirin. But he was still agitated. Pacing and going to the door.

"You know what I think?" I said.

"What's that?"

"I think he wants to go hunting."

"After *that*?"

"Pain is something you forget. We've got an hour of daylight left; want to give it a try?"

So we got back in the truck and headed to a place I knew that was close to the house. We unloaded and Jeb waited, patiently, for me to buckle the collar on his neck. Then, when I said, "Hunt 'em up," he took off, full of his old enthusiasm.

"What do you suppose will happen if he runs into another porcupine?" Marsha asked.

"Well, I've always heard that when it comes to porcupines, there are two kinds of dogs. After the first encounter, one kind of dog says, 'Man, that's it. I'm never getting close to another one of those things as long as I live.'"

"And the other kind?"

"He says, 'I'm going to get even. From now on, I kill every one of those dudes I see.' Which category do you think Jeb will fall into?"

"I don't think there is any question about it," Marsha said. "So why don't you ask me a hard one."

FOURTEEN

We didn't run into any more porcupines that season, but Jeb did, indeed, turn out to belong to that second category of dog. I started wearing one of those multipurpose tools on my belt, and on several occasions—I've actually lost track of how many—I had to stop in the field and spend an hour pulling quills from his mouth and muzzle. I never could decide which was more remarkable: the fact that he couldn't get it through his head that porcupines were something to leave alone, or his stoicism when I pulled those quills. Inevitably, when the job was finished and both of us looked like we'd been in a bad bar fight, and lost, he would take off and start hunting again like nothing had happened.

The porcupine encounters were good for a story, anyway, and my wife and daughters and I enjoyed telling stories about Jeb. John Hann may have turned him into a capable bird dog, but he was still an incorrigible adolescent. If there was trouble around somewhere, Jeb would find a way to get into it. He reminded me of that wonderful old Bill Cosby line: "He's a good boy. It's just that I couldn't think of enough things to tell him not to do."

Jeb ran away and came home green. He dug up flower beds and knocked over garbage cans. He tunneled out of the kennel I built for him. Rolled in all manner of smelly things. He made a mess of things in ways you could never have predicted.

For instance, there was the time when my wife invited some friends over for dinner. These were second-home people, up for the fall colors, and they tended to be more formal than those of us who lived in Vermont full-time. One of the women arrived wearing a fine white designer dress.

Well, it was a Saturday, during the tenderloin of bird season, and Jeb and I had been out all day. We'd had some success and, as usual, when Jeb was finding birds, he pushed himself. On this occasion, he spent a lot of time plowing through thick briars. His tail was moving all the time and the briars had worn it raw and bloody. When he wagged his tail, it left bloody stripes on his flank so that it looked like he'd been flogged for mutiny or something. At the end of the day, I cleaned him up with warm, soapy water and put some ointment on the raw, wounded tip of his tail to help it heal. Then, I put him out in the kennel (which had a cement floor, by now) to keep him out of the way during Marsha's dinner party.

One of our guests was a casual bird hunter. When everyone had just arrived and we were making conversation, it came up that I'd been out that day. This man asked how I'd done.

"We had a good day," I said. "Got two grouse and should have had two more."

"Who is 'we'?" he said.

"Me and Jeb Stuart," I said. "My dog."

"Oh yeah? What breed is he?"

"A pointer."

"Never met anybody up here before who hunts with pointers," he said.

"It is a little unusual," I said. "But I always wanted one."

"And he's pretty good?"

"Yes," I said, modestly, "he does all right."

"Is he around? I'd like to see him."

"Well . . . I don't know. He's in the kennel right now, and, you know, he's kind of excitable."

"Oh, bring him in," Marsha said. She was as fond of Jeb as I, and liked to show him off.

"Maybe another time . . . "

"Come on," Marsha said. "Just for a minute. Then you can take him back out to the kennel."

The other guests said they would like to meet Jeb, and without much more prodding—and any thought at all—I said I'd bring him in.

So Jeb joined the party, wagging his tail furiously the way he does when he meets new people. A scab had begun to form on his tail where he'd rubbed it raw, but when his tail hit the leg of a chair, hard, the wound opened up. After that, every swish of Jeb's tail sent a shower of blood droplets across the room. It was like a lawn sprinkler that you couldn't turn off. In an instant, the lady in the white dress looked like she had been cast in a Mafia movie. There were blood spots the size of half dollars from her hemline to her neck. The rest of us got some, too, but she got the full effect.

Everyone started scrambling to get out of the line of fire, and the excitement just made Jeb wag his tail more energetically. The white walls of the dining room and the pale yellow tablecloth were splattered, along with the wineglasses, the curtains, the rug, and everything else that was in range.

"*Get him, Geoffrey!*" Marsha shouted, and I did. I hustled Jeb back out to the kennel and returned looking like I'd gone ten rounds with Roy Jones. The woman in the white dress was dabbing at it forlornly with a clean, wet sponge, but it was hopeless.

I apologized profusely for my dog, though it wasn't really his fault. It was an honorable wound, I thought, and he'd gotten it working hard to find birds . . . for me. Still, we made all the right noises about dropping by in the morning to pick up the dress and taking it to the cleaners, but we all knew that was a nonstarter. That little item from Adrienne Vittadini was now a very expensive rag.

The best part was, it was still early. In the old "the show must go on" spirit, I served drinks, we sat around for hors d'oeuvres, and then took our places at the table for dinner. It could have been the mess tent at a MASH unit, but we all carried on as though nothing was amiss. The woman in the white dress, especially, brought the whole thing off beautifully, and that couldn't have been easy. She complimented my wife on the dinner, and when she was told we were eating grouse, she raised her glass to Jeb, saying a meal like this was easily worth a frock. After all, you could always buy a new dress, but they weren't serving grouse at any of the restaurants she knew. When she was leaving and I was, once again, apologizing, she waved it off and said, "You know, that is some dog you've got there. And I'll say this for him. He sure knows how to make an entrance."

After a year or two, even Marsha was able to laugh at the story.

So Jeb was our house comedian and the source of many treasured family memories. A lot of conversations at the dinner table started with the line, "Do you remember the time when Jeb . . ."

And we would listen to the tale, once again. Families, it seems to me, build a fund of memories and then live for years off the interest. Jeb gave high returns on the investment.

He was a bird dog by breeding and training but he was a family dog by nature. He was always ready for whatever we were doing. If we were out in the yard in the fall, raking leaves, Jeb would be out there with us. If we wanted to go for a long hike up in the hills beyond the house, then he wanted to go, too, though a couple of those excursions were cut short by porcupine encounters. If asked, he would ride with you to the grocery store. He even went on a couple of cross-country skiing trips, but being a short-haired dog, he got pretty cold and we decided that it might be prudent to leave him at home when the snow was deep. He would howl mournfully when we left, and we could hear him all the way to the end of the drive.

During the summer, when he wasn't finding manure piles to roll in and turn himself green, he would chase things in the back meadow. Everything from grasshoppers to moles. He mounted a campaign against the squirrels that plundered our bird feeders, and while he never even came close to catching one, he never gave up either. He was high-spirited, fearless, and undaunted by failure or pain. He was a full-out kind of guy, and it gave you a lift just being around him. He was one of those dogs that, when you were feeling low, he could change your mood and bring you up.

There were successes in the field, of course, and if he had simply been a good bird dog, that would have been enough for me. But as one of my friends once said (about another dog, actually), "He isn't in it to be a success. Any dog can do that. What he wants to do is create a legend."

My daughters were especially fond of old Jeb. Brooke went away to prep school a couple of years after Jeb became part of the family, and when she called home, she would always ask about him. When she came home for a weekend or on vacation, Jeb would give her the cold shoulder for the first hour or two she was in the house. He wanted to make sure she understood that he knew she'd abandoned him, and he didn't like it one little bit.

"Come on, buddy," she would say. "I can't help it. I'm sorry. Please come here."

Jeb would sit across the room, with his back turned, ignoring her pleadings. But after a while, he would soften and come when she called him, and, eventually, he would climb up in her lap and all would be forgiven.

One year it was time to go on the dreaded (by me, anyway) tour of colleges. Brooke had several places in mind, and they had one thing in common: they were all located in large, urban areas. She'd had enough of small, cute New England towns. So, one weekend, we drove down to Washington, D.C., so she could visit Georgetown.

"You know," I said, "we could take an extra day and walk the battlefield at Gettysburg. It's right on the way."

She was reading American history that year and agreed eagerly.

On the drive down, we listened to a taped reading of Michael Shaara's novel, *The Killer Angels*. The book is a moment-by-moment account of the Gettysburg battle, and in my view, the fictional masterpiece of the Civil War. I figured it would be an excellent preparation for Brooke before we walked the battlefield, and a good way to pass time on the highway. Better, certainly, than listening to Nine Inch Nails and her other musical favorites.

Well into the narrative, and more than six hours into our drive, the historical J.E.B. Stuart, Confederate cavalry general, appears. He has been missed by Robert E. Lee, who had been depending on him to keep track of the Union Army's movements. Stuart had been off riding and raiding the countryside, looking for headlines, while Lee blundered into a battle he did not want, on ground that was not of his choosing. Historians consider Stuart's absence from the battlefield in the days before Pickett's charge as one of the principal reasons for the outcome.

Shaara described Stuart (and the reader on the tape delivered it beautifully) this way:

> The cavalier, a beautiful man, was lounging against a fence, a white rail fence, in a circle of light, a circle of admirers. Reporters were taking notes. Stuart was dressed in soft gray with butternut braid along the arms and around the collar and lace at his throat, and the feathered hat was swept back to hang happily, boyishly from the back of the head, and curls peeked out across the wide handsome forehead. Full-bearded, to hide a weak chin, but a lovely boy, carefree, mud-spattered, obviously tired, languid, cheery, confident . . . he gave the impression of having been up for days, in the saddle for days, and not minding it.

Brooke laughed for five minutes. "That's perfect, Dad," she said. "He's got just the right name."

Since Brooke was away, first at prep school and then at college, Hadley and Marsha spent more time in the field with Jeb than she did. And they both went out, I think, not so much to shoot birds as to watch Jeb. I believe that a big part of their fascination was in seeing this dog that they thought of as a comic at home perform with such serious intensity in the field. When it came to birds, Jeb was all business . . . until he came across a porcupine, anyway.

Hadley had always been keen on animals—she still worked with Jeb and her Lab just because she enjoyed doing it—and loved the outdoors. She knew the trees and could identify birds, and she had a fantastic pair of eyes. "Look at the deer," she would say, and I would strain to see what she was pointing at and, after a while, make out the shape, obscured in the shadows.

She also liked to eat what we killed, and was especially fond of woodcock, which is a mature, refined taste. The woodcock's diet is made up almost exclusively of earthworms. The bird flies great distances so its breast meat is very dark, unlike the grouse, which walks more than it flies and has white breast meat. The woodcock tastes something like liver and something like duck, and has a flavor that is unique and not for everyone. But Hadley loves it, and when the flight birds were in, she would go out with me for the last hour of daylight after she got home from school.

When she started changing from running shoes to boots in the kitchen, Jeb would know what was up and start doing his manic act. He would bark and tear around the house, balling up the rugs and digging his toenails into the soft pine boards on the kitchen floor. We repeatedly refinished the floor because of those grooves.

"You ready to get them, buddy?" Hadley would say to Jeb, getting him more and more pumped, until it seemed like he just couldn't stand it. We'd open the door and Jeb would race outside and take a position next to the pickup, waiting for her to open the door. He would sit on her lap on the way to whatever covert we were hunting that day, moaning the whole way.

"You think the flight birds will be in?" Hadley would say to him. "We had a full moon last night, so they should have been flying. What do you think, Jeb?"

And Jeb would moan.

If the birds were in, Jeb would find them. Since woodcock are fairly slow fliers and generally go straight up and give you a clear, unobstructed shot (unlike grouse), I could hit them. The limit was three, and when the flight birds were in, I often filled mine. Hadley had not yet started shooting—that came later—but three birds was enough for dinner.

We would clean the birds and feed the dogs when we got home, and then help Marsha make dinner. She cooked the woodcock in the oven, with strips of bacon over the breast, until they were warm to the bone but still very rare. This is the way we all liked them, but it was a little disconcerting to look across the table at my beautiful baby daughter gnawing at the red, dripping carcass of a small bird. While her sister had become a vegetarian at prep school, Hadley remained a true carnivore.

She was also a great companion, and I realized during those times how much I would one day miss them. There were things on the near horizon that were going to take her away from me. She would be getting her driver's license soon, and then, there were boys. I knew that even when I shot a limit of woodcock, I couldn't compete.

So I tried to make the most of the time that was left, and we had some wonderful days in the field together. Jeb was a part of it, and part of a lot of other things, too. There were times, riding home in the early dark, after an evening hunting birds with Hadley, when I thought about how close I had come to giving the dog away and missing all of this. It seemed impossible.

FIFTEEN

When it came time for Hadley to go on the college tour, she was looking at art schools. There was one in Georgia and another in Boston, which sounded good to me since it was close; an easy bus ride would get her home. Brooke was attending the University of Chicago, and it seemed we seldom saw her. I liked the idea of having at least one of my girls around, if only for some weekends during bird season.

Hadley was also looking at a school in Kansas City. It had a good reputation and, even better, after looking at some samples of Hadley's work, the school had offered her a fairly substantial scholarship. She wanted to go out and take a look.

So I called Ted Hatfield, who had moved to Kansas City from St. Joseph, Missouri.

"Great," he said. "Will she be by herself, or will you be coming along?"

"Me or Marsha," I said. "One of us ought to get a look at the place."

"Well, why don't you come? Make it in October and bring Jeb along. I'm sure his old buddy, John Hann, will be glad to see him, and I know where we can hunt some birds while Hadley is taking her tour."

"Talked me right into it," I said.

Hadley liked the plan, too, except for the fact that she would not be able to go hunting with Ted, me, and Jeb.

"Well, if you decide to go to school there, Jeb and I will come visit," I told her. "And if the bird hunting is as good as Ted Hatfield has told me it is, then you'll be seeing a lot of us."

If Hadley and I were excited about the trip, Jeb was the other thing. He'd had only the one experience flying—to John Hann's and back—and that one hadn't gone at all well. When I'd put him in his crate that time, he'd begun howling. I don't know how long he kept it up, but he was still howling when I walked away from the crate on the loading dock. He'd howled, again, on our return from Missouri, and when the airline baggage handler put the crate on the conveyor and it disappeared behind the wall, he was still howling. On that return flight, I'd thought I could hear him crying, down in the baggage compartment, but I couldn't be sure given the engine noise. Probably, I thought, it was just my overwrought, sympathetic, guilty imagination.

Anyway, I'd told myself, Jeb was a dog and he would get over it. And, plainly, he did. There were no lasting traumas. Still, we wanted to make things easy for him, so Hadley let him sit in her lap all the way to the airport, and then she sat with him and patted him in the terminal while I did the paperwork to get him on our flight from Albany to Kansas City.

Jeb was apprehensive, and several people in the airport approached him and made nice and complimented Hadley on what a handsome dog he was. Jeb had always liked attention, so that diverted him and calmed him down a little.

But when it came time to get in the crate, and the door was shut, he set up a cry that you could hear all through the airport. The crate went on the conveyor belt, and as it moved away, I could see Jeb looking at us beseechingly through the small wire window as he howled piteously.

"He'll be all right, don't you worry," a woman in the ticket line said to Hadley, who was almost as upset as Jeb.

"Thank you," Hadley said. "I know he will. But he just sounds so *sad*."

We got our boarding passes and had time for coffee. I tried to reassure Hadley while we sat at the little table.

"I'll bet he settled down just as soon as he couldn't see us anymore."

"I hope so," she said, sipping her latte and still looking concerned.

"It's like when we put him in the kennel at home because we have to run an errand. He makes a big scene, but when you come back, he's stretched out on his pillow, sound asleep."

"I guess."

We boarded early and found our seats. I looked out the window while the baggage was being loaded and watched as Jeb's crate was put on the conveyor and slowly made its way toward the belly of the big machine.

"There he is," I said to Hadley, "I see him."

And, a minute later, I could hear him, too. So could all the other passengers on that flight. Jeb's howls made it up from the baggage compartment, sounding almost like the nocturnal laments of a wolf.

The woman who had reassured Hadley in the ticket line came down the aisle and when she saw us, she bent down and said, "I still think he'll be all right. We had a dog like that, once. Don't worry."

Hadley smiled wanly and said, "Thank you."

The people in the seats around us now knew that those sounds of woe coming up from the baggage compartment were from our dog. We got several sideways looks and a few people shook their heads disapprovingly. Now Hadley was embarrassed.

"Forget it," I said. "People bring screaming babies and misbehaving kids on airplanes all the time."

Hadley nodded and hid her face behind a book.

The pilot finally powered up and if Jeb was still howling, we couldn't hear it over the engine noise. Not, anyway, until we arrived at our gate in Kansas City and the engines spooled down. There was no mistaking the sound from the baggage hold.

"There he is," Hadley said. "I wonder if he kept that up the whole way?"

"I wouldn't doubt it."

We took Jeb out of his crate as soon as we retrieved it, and in a couple of minutes, it was as though nothing had happened. The experience had been unpleasant, to say the least, but he recovered quickly. He strained at his leash and wagged his tail when strangers stopped to pat him, and generally behaved as though nothing had happened and it was a fine day to be alive and in Kansas City.

"I really don't get him sometimes," I said.

"*Sometimes?*" Hadley said.

Ted Hatfield had arranged some bird hunting on a couple of farms outside of St. Joseph, and on our way to one of them, we would drive past John Hann's house and place of business.

"You mind if we stop?" I said.

"Not at all. I'm sure John will be glad to see Jeb. The feeling might even be mutual."

John was just getting started with the string of dogs he would be training that day, but he took a minute to talk. He asked how Jeb had been doing and I said, "Fine. Just fine. I've slacked off a little on him, let him get away with more than you would have."

Jeb, as if to confirm the truth of that observation, took the opportunity to slip away from us. I'd told him to "stay," and at first, he'd remained at my side while John and Ted and I talked. But now, he wanted to check out the sights and, especially, the smells.

John Hann barely turned his head and said, "Jeb. Where do you think you're going?"

Jeb stopped, turned, and came back to where he'd been standing. He took his position and hardly moved a muscle.

"Hasn't forgotten that voice, has he?" Hatfield said.

We asked John if he wanted to go along with us. He said thanks, but he was too busy, so we loaded Jeb back in the truck and went on down the road to the first farm we would be hunting.

"How about that?" I said. "Hann didn't even raise his voice and Jeb snapped to like a Marine in boot camp."

"Yeah," Hatfield said. "Don't you just love it when a pointer has good manners?"

There was a lot of good-looking ground on the farm where Ted had permission for us to hunt. Acres and acres that had been set aside in the government Conservation Reserve Program. More ground than Jeb and I hunted in a week back home, and all of it brand new. He had fallen into velvet and seemed to realize it. As soon as I'd put the collar on him and told him to "hunt 'em up," he took off, running out ahead of us, coursing the ground like the old pro he was becoming. It was a clear morning with the ground still damp and no wind to speak of. Perfect scenting conditions and easy walking.

"This is pretty fine, Ted," I said.

"Worth the trip?"

"Every bit, I'd say."

"Well, let's reserve judgment until we've found some birds. There are both pheasants and quail on this place. More pheasants, I'm afraid."

"Be a new experience for Jeb," I said. "He's never pointed one of them."

We made conversation as we walked through the wet, knee-high grass. This is one of the rewards of hunting with a dog that doesn't require constant minding. Since your entire focus is no longer on the dog, you can relax a little and enjoy the company of your hunting partner and the sensations of a day in the field. You can study the ground and listen to the birds and fall into a rhythm and a reverie that is one of the ineffable joys of upland hunting. By now, Jeb had done enough of this that he knew the drill. He covered the ground, stayed in range, and checked back in pretty much without being told. Ted and I were free to talk. It was bird hunting as it was meant to be.

An hour after we'd started, we came to an east-facing hillside where the sun had dried the grass and the air was noticeably warmer than it had been in the lower country, which we had hunted pretty thoroughly without finding anything more than a couple of rabbits. Jeb had been tempted, but he didn't chase them.

"Likely pheasant spot," Ted said.

And almost as he said it, Jeb stopped and came to a point.

"He's on," I said.

"Okay. Let's move in on him."

A hen pheasant got up in front of Jeb, in easy range. When we didn't shoot (only roosters are legal), Jeb looked confused.

"It's okay, bud," I said. "Find another."

I had to tap him on the head to release him, and before he'd gone another twenty steps, he was on point again. Another hen flushed in easy gun range.

I released him again and he moved on up the slope, cat-footing it now. He wasn't sure about this. The birds were unfamiliar, and for some reason, nobody seemed to want to shoot one.

When we reached the crest of the little hill, he stopped again. When the pheasant he was pointing flushed, another bird came up a few feet from the first one. And then another. And another. Bird after bird. Mostly hens, but a few roosters, too—though all of them were out of range when they came out of the grass. There must have been thirty pheasants concealing themselves in the warm, dry grass on that little hillside. Jeb had never seen so many birds. Might not see that many grouse flush at close range in an entire season. It was a riot of birds, and if he'd come off point and started chasing them, I wouldn't have blamed him or even spoken sternly to him. Some provocations are just too much to resist.

But Jeb stayed staunch and was still there, holding his ground, after the last bird had flushed and flown down the long slope on the back side of the hill.

"Man," I said. "I wish John Hann had seen that."

Jeb was bewildered but still game when we left that little hill to hunt for more birds. I couldn't believe we'd find any. I figured we'd flushed every bird on that farm in about thirty seconds of action.

But a half hour or so later, Jeb came to a point on a grown-over fence line. He was solid and I said, "I believe there has to be a bird in there. Or maybe a whole covey of them."

"Well, let's take opposite sides of the fence and go in on him."

We did, and when I was almost at Jeb's side a cock pheasant came out of the grass with the loud, characteristic squawk, its wings beating furiously. The bird flew to Ted's side of the fence and he let it get out just a little before he shot. When he did, the bird crumpled and hit the ground with a thud. It was a clean, conclusive shot, and a second later, everything seemed very quiet.

Jeb stood steady, the way John Hann had taught him. I wasn't an absolute stickler for this at home. If he ran to the bird once I'd shot, I didn't correct him. He had kept a number of crippled grouse from getting away in the brush by going immediately after them. It wasn't perfect "steady to wing and shot" form, but it was okay with me. But maybe because he'd seen John Hann that morning, and been brought up sternly by him, Jeb was remembering his lessons.

I tapped him on the head. "Okay, man. Hunt dead."

He broke from the pose and ran straight to the dead bird, picked it up in his mouth, and returned it to Ted.

"Thanks, Jeb," Ted said. "But how did you know I was the one who shot it?"

"Too good a shot for it to have been me."

"No, no. He's just a very aware dog."

We hunted that farm for the rest of the morning and put up a few more pheasant, mostly hens. Then, when it was getting on toward lunchtime and my boots were starting to feel heavy, Jeb hit a point in the middle of a little field of no particular distinction. When we had moved up to his side, Jeb broke off the point and took a few careful steps before locking up again.

"That bird is running on him," Ted said. "Pheasant are bad about that."

"Can't be any worse than grouse. He's learned how to trail them."

"Well, we need to keep up with him. Sooner or later, that bird will have to fly."

We walked in on seven or eight points. Each time, Jeb would break and trail the bird, moving with the stealth of a burglar on the job. Finally, we reached a little tractor trail. Instead of crossing bare ground, the pheasant flew. It was another rooster, and this time, it flew to my side. I missed with the first barrel but not the second.

Jeb brought my bird in and I thanked and praised him effusively.

It was the first pheasant of our partnership, and that seemed important in some way. Jeb was out of a line of dogs bred for quail hunting, and so far in his career, we had never shot one. He'd pointed that covey in John Hann's field, back when I'd come to pick him up and get some instruction myself. But there had been no shooting. Since then, he'd pointed woodcock and grouse back in Vermont, and I'd shot a few. Now, he'd added pheasant to the repertoire. I saw virtue in his versatility. Still, I wondered how he'd do on quail if we did find any.

We stopped for lunch, which meant getting back in the truck and driving a couple of miles to a convenience store where we bought sodas and sandwiches. I gave Jeb half my sandwich and he inhaled it. Then I filled a bowl with water from an outside faucet and he drank that. The morning had warmed steadily and it was hot now. I was tired, but Jeb did not seem to be. While Ted and I sat on the tailgate of the pickup, finishing lunch, Jeb paced around the bed like he couldn't wait to get going again.

"Lie down, bud," I said. "You'll get more chances."

"I believe he likes Missouri hunting."

"Well, he's never hunted so much country. So he probably feels like I've finally given him his reins and let him run the way the Lord intended him to."

"He does like to cover some ground, doesn't he?"

"Lives for it."

"Bless his heart."

We went back to the farm to hunt out a large piece we hadn't covered that morning. It was much warmer now, and walking was much slower. Everything felt heavier—my boots, the shells in my vest, and, especially, my eyelids. Ted and I didn't talk much, merely trudged silently across a wide CRP field, watching Jeb as he moved back and forth, looking for scent.

Then, in an instant, the monotony was broken.

"Got us a point," Ted said.

We were slightly above Jeb, on a long, sloping piece of ground. He was about fifty yards ahead of us and locked onto the closest thing I'd seen to a classic point all day.

His neck was stretched taut, his tail was straight, and one of his forelegs was off the ground and cocked. I was sorry I hadn't brought my camera. At that moment I'd rather have had a photograph than a shot.

We moved in, and when we were a few steps beyond Jeb, who held his ground, quivering just slightly, a covey of about twenty quail broke out of the grass in a simultaneous explosion of small, brown feathered projectiles.

No matter how many times you've experienced it, there is something so startling about that first moment of a covey rise that you feel screwed into the ground, immobilized.

I took a moment, but I got the gun to my shoulder and tracked the outside bird on my side. When I caught up with him, I touched the trigger and the bird fell. I tried to shift to another but I wasn't quick and fluid enough, and didn't get another shot. I watched the singles fly on, fanning out across the slope and dropping, one by one, into the grass.

"How'd you do?" Ted said.

"One. How about you?"

"I believe I got a double," he said. "And, man, wasn't *that* a nice piece of dog work?"

"Yes," I said, and purely loved saying it. "It was real nice dog work."

I would have taken a minute to shower Jeb with *attaboys*, but he didn't have time for that. He was a pro now, and he had work to do.

So as soon as I released him from the point, he retrieved the three downed birds. When he'd brought the third one in, he stood at my side, quivering. He'd marked those singles, too, and wanted to get after them.

"Do we hunt them?" I said to Ted. Sometimes you hunt the singles and sometimes you leave them for seed. We'd taken three birds out of the covey, and I thought that might be enough. But these were Jeb's first quail and I wanted him to keep going . . . almost as much as he did.

"I think we can take another two or three. It was a pretty big covey."

"Okay, Jeb. Hunt close, now, bud. Hunt close."

He moved off, down the slope, looking more alert and moving more carefully than before he'd found the covey. And before long, he'd pointed one of the singles.

I shot that bird and Jeb retrieved it. When I released him, he went back to work, looking like he could not get enough.

On the next point, two birds got up. They flew to Ted's side, and I watched as he mounted the gun with a kind of fluid, graceful ease, almost nonchalance, tracked them, and brought both of them down with one shot.

I couldn't remember the last time I'd seen that.

"*Great* shot," I said.

"Lucky," he said. "Even a blind pig finds an acorn, every now and then."

"I figure you just brought me out here to show off, right?"

"No. But I will be asking you to sign an affidavit, saying you witnessed it."

Jeb brought the birds in and we decided to leave the rest for seed. When we moved off in another direction, away from the remaining singles, Jeb gave me a look of utter bewilderment.

Boss Man, it seemed to say, *are you nuts or something? Things are just now getting good.*

But we had a nice bag. Two pheasants and six quail. We didn't find any more birds that afternoon, and when we quit, we were all tired. Jeb climbed into the truck and went promptly to sleep. He did it in a way that seemed to say he'd done a good day's work and had earned his rest. Now, what was for dinner?

I gave him some canned food—a reward he devoured like he hadn't eaten in a week. Ted, his wife, his daughter, Hadley, and I ate pheasant and quail for our dinner, and it was a fine, fitting end to a good day. Hadley said she'd had a good day, too, and I wanted to know how the college tour had gone, but she was more interested in hearing how Jeb had performed. So, without much reluctance, Ted and I relived our day in the field, making sure to talk up all of Jeb's triumphs. Hadley seemed even prouder of Jeb than I was. She had always believed in him.

"Now, aren't you glad you didn't give him away?" she said.

"I can't believe I ever considered it."

We left the next morning, early, and if Jeb hadn't had reason to feel paranoid about air travel before this trip, then the flight home gave him strong cause never to want to fly again. We went through what was, by now, the usual howling when we loaded him into his box and sent him on his way down the conveyor. Hadley seemed almost as distressed as he was. The only thing I could say to reassure her was, "He'll get over it."

We boarded the plane, and it was a relief when the engines spooled up and we couldn't hear him, down in the baggage compartment, any longer.

The pilot taxied out and firewalled the engines for takeoff. He accelerated down the runway and, then, about halfway to liftoff, powered back and stood on the reverse thrusters and breaks, aborting the takeoff. Passengers looked at each other and out of the windows with the kind of concern you'd expect. There was no smell of smoke or sign of fire. When the plane was taxiing back to the gate, the pilot came on and told us, in that reassuring voice they all must master, "Ladies and gentlemen, as you can tell, we have a little problem . . . "

Always a *little* problem.

This one, he went on, was probably just an instrument light, nothing serious, and so on and so forth. "But we're going back in to get it checked out. We can't tell you, yet, how long the delay will be."

Three or four hours, as it turned out.

The passengers all got out and milled around the gate, checking with clerks on their connections. The baggage—and Jeb—stayed aboard. We couldn't hear him howling, but I suspect the technicians who were looking for the source of the problem could.

We finally reboarded and taxied out for another try.

Power up and rolling. Then, halfway down the runway, another screaming abort, and back to the gate. The pilot's tone was not so soothing this time. If the passengers were alarmed, he was irritated . . . and more.

There was no third try, probably because if there had been, it would have been with an empty airplane. The baggage was unloaded and the passengers were all courteously rebooked.

By now, Hadley and I had missed all possible connections to Albany, so the airline made arrangements to put us up for the night and get us out on the first available flight in the morning. We gathered up our bags—and Jeb—and loaded into a motel shuttle. Jeb was trembling, and the driver kindly let us take him out of the box so he could sit in Hadley's lap during the ride.

The motel was nice enough. But it was the only structure on a brand-new interstate exchange. No restaurants and no convenience stores.

"Did you bring any food for Jeb?" Hadley asked.

"No. Just a couple of extra dog biscuits that I keep in my vest for treats."

"That won't be enough. Not anywhere near."

"I know."

"Well, what are we going to do?"

"We've got to eat, too, right?"

"Yes."

"Do you feel like pizza?"

"Sure."

"Look in that phone book, then, and see if there's a Domino's, or something like that. We'll order two pizzas. One for us and one for Jeb."

"Cool."

"What do you think he'll want on his?"

"Sausage?"

"Works for me."

So we ordered two pizzas and asked that the one with sausage be cooked first and allowed to cool a little before they started the other one. When they arrived, we made sure that Jeb's was cool enough so he wouldn't burn his mouth on it. When we opened the lid of the box and put it on the floor, Jeb looked at the pizza and then he looked at us. We were pretty strict with him at home about eating off our plates, so he wasn't entirely sure about this deal.

"Go ahead, bud," I said, "knock yourself out."

He was still reluctant.

So I tore a little piece off the pizza and fed it to him by hand. He devoured it and licked his lips.

"Likes that oregano taste, doesn't he?" I said to Hadley.

"I think it's the cheese, Dad."

This time, when I pointed at the pizza on the floor, Jeb didn't hesitate. He put his face down into the little cardboard box and came up only for air. When he was finished, his muzzle was smeared red with tomato sauce so he looked like he was wearing lipstick.

Hadley and I hadn't finished ours, and he looked like he wouldn't mind if we fed him a scrap or two from it.

"He's had a hard day," I said. "We can give him some of the crust."

He ate that, too. Then, probably because the pizza was salty, he went in the bathroom and drank the toilet dry.

Jeb slept soundly while Hadley and I watched an NFL game, and in the morning, with the usual reluctance and howling, he was loaded onto another airplane. This one made it off the ground and we had a routine flight home. Hadley and I now had a new Jeb story to add to the family fund, and we've told it many, many times since. And, except for the histrionics about flying, the trip had been a success. I found myself hoping that Hadley would decide on the school in Kansas City. I saw many fine fall weekends in the Missouri countryside in our future.

SIXTEEN

Hadley chose the school in Boston over the one in Kansas City. But that was okay, I told myself, since she could make it home weekends, and during bird season we would go out together. And Jeb would be happy with that, too, since nobody had ever treated him better than Hadley, and he lavishly repaid her in affection.

It worked out fine in Hadley's first year at school, and I was looking forward to her sophomore year when we had a setback.

Marsha was diagnosed with cancer, and in that instant, bird hunting, along with everything else, went onto a far back burner. Hadley wanted to stay home and be with her mother while she was recovering from surgery and going through chemo. But I persuaded her, barely, to go on back to Boston.

"Just come home as often as you can. It'll mean a lot to your mom."

"I'll be here every weekend, Dad."

"I sort of thought you would."

She rode the bus every Friday afternoon and got in late, after dinner. She would spend Saturday and Sunday morning with us, and then catch a bus back to Boston a little after noon. It was a lot of dreary time on the highway—more than four hours each way—but it was a comfort to Marsha, having her around, and probably more than that to me. I looked forward to picking Hadley up at the bus stop Friday night and always felt better when I saw the big coach make the turn and then come to a stop. The doors would open and I would look for her face and wave when I saw her. She would smile when she saw me, and it was the same smile I remembered from the time she was a baby, dimples and all. But I could see the strain behind it. We were all trying hard.

Too hard, probably, for Marsha, who was dealing with the chemo by not giving in to the symptoms or to anything else that came with having cancer, including losing her hair. She resisted—no, *resented*—being fawned over and treated like some kind of "sick person," and if you laid anything even close to pity on her, she wouldn't tolerate it. Hadley and I learned not to ask her how she felt because the answer was always, "I'm *fine*." Even when you could see she wasn't.

Marsha, as much as possible, did not want to change the way she did things just because she had what she called "this crappy disease." There were concessions, of course, but every one was made reluctantly, almost defiantly. And part of this total-war approach was to insist that nobody else change the way they did things, either. She was like the wonderful character, Hank Stamper, in the Ken Kesey novel, *Sometimes a Great Notion*, whose mantra in life was, "Never give an inch."

So it was no big surprise when she said—on a Friday night after I'd picked Hadley up at the bus stop and we were sitting around talking—"Tomorrow is opening day of grouse season, isn't it? Doesn't it always fall on the last Saturday of September?"

"That's right," I said.

"Well, you two are going out in the morning, right?"

"Oh, I don't know . . . "

"Of course you are. It wouldn't be fair to Jeb to miss it."

"Mom . . . " Hadley said.

"Try to bring home some birds. We'll have grouse for dinner." She was having trouble keeping food down, but never mind.

"Are you sure . . . "

"It's opening day, isn't it? And you have to go out on opening day."

There was no arguing with that logic. Or with her.

So Hadley and I got up early and dressed for opening day, to Jeb's great delight. Dog lovers have a weakness for anthropomorphizing, and I am as guilty as any. Still, I was certain that Jeb had picked up on the mood in the house, which had changed even if Marsha had resisted changing anything. He seemed to need more affection and to stay closer than usual. He moved restlessly around the house, checking on things, and when Marsha was in bed, resting, he would find a place where he could lie down and watch her. There was something in the air and he sensed it. I believe that firmly.

But he was still a bird dog, and unlike the human animal, he knew exactly what he'd been put on earth to do. So that Saturday morning, when he saw me putting on my briarproof pants, he went into his act of tearing around the house, bunching up all the rugs, digging his claws into the soft wood of the kitchen floor, and barking like he'd suddenly gone mad.

"Settle down, Jeb," I said. Which was like telling the wind to lie down and stop blowing.

I let him out so I could finish dressing in peace.

"He's eager," Marsha said. "Even if you aren't."

"I'm eager. I just wish you could go with us."

"I'll go next year. That's a promise."

Hadley and I went to all our favorite places and Jeb found a few birds, but the leaves were still thick on the trees and we heard more birds than we saw. I missed one makeable shot and apologized to Hadley and to Jeb.

"It's been a long time since I've done any shooting. I stopped the gun. I must have been five yards behind that bird. Sorry."

"That's okay, Dad," Hadley said.

Jeb was less tolerant. He gave me the look I'd seen many times before that said, *Hey man, I'm busting my chops here. You've got to do your part.*

151

So we came home empty-handed but happy. It had been a good day in the field—aren't they all?—and it took our minds off the other thing. Most of the time, at least.

"That was fun, Dad," Hadley said. "Thanks for taking me."

"Thank you, kid," I said. "I never do any good on opening day, anyway."

"Well, in a couple of weeks the flight birds will be coming in. I can almost taste those woodcock."

And, sure enough, three weekends later, the flight birds arrived. I knew this from my bird-hunting friends who called with reports of many birds pointed, some shot, and general good things going on in the coverts we all hunted. I wasn't getting out during the week; there was just too much going on at home. But I looked forward to Hadley's arrival.

She came in by bus on Friday night, as usual, looking wan but trying hard not to. We were all playing by Marsha Rules. Never give an inch. We played cards that night in front of a fire in the fireplace. Three-handed hearts, and it was a spirited game.

After the last hand, Marsha said, "You two need to get to bed. You'll want to get an early start. I want a limit of woodcock for dinner tomorrow night."

Hadley didn't have a license and wouldn't be carrying a gun, so that meant three birds. One apiece for dinner.

That part turned out to be easy. There were plenty of birds in the coverts, Jeb pointed them like it was a routine job of work, and my shooting was better than it usually is. By mid-morning, I had my limit of woodcock, and we stopped hunting in the places where we knew there would probably be woodcock and went looking for grouse. By late afternoon, I'd managed to get three of them, as well. It was about as productive a day as I've ever had in the field.

So we returned in triumph. Marsha praised her "providers" fulsomely, and started looking up recipes for a risotto that she thought would compliment the woodcock nicely.

"You sure you want to cook?" I said cautiously. Kitchen smells often brought on an attack of nausea that was a match for even her strong will.

"I'll be *fine*," she said.

So we brushed Jeb out and picked a couple of ticks off him. Then we rewarded him with a dinner of canned food. Gave him the whole can, which he ate without coming up for air. When he was finished, he sighed and retired to a spot in front of the fire and fell into the sleep of the just. Hadley kept me company while I drew and plucked our birds.

"You know what I think I'm going to do?" I said as I worked.

"What's that?"

"I believe I'm going to save these grouse. Put them in the freezer until Thanksgiving—no, Christmas. Mom's chemo will be done by then, I think, and we'll cook a big meal. Grouse, wild rice, acorn squash, mince pie. It will be a celebration. I'll get some decent wine and a good bottle of champagne."

"That sounds great, but you'll have to get one more grouse because Brooke (who had abandoned vegetarianism) will be home and we'll need one bird for each person."

"Don't you worry about that," I said. "I'll explain the situation to Jeb and he'll make sure we get that bird."

By the time the birds were ready for the oven, Marsha's risotto was on the stove and our little kitchen was filling with its dark aromas; a blend of the spices, stock, mushrooms, and something that came from the mingling of all of them. If you were hungry—and Hadley and I were—then it was a fragrance to make your mouth water and your head feel a little light.

With Marsha, however, it did another thing. I could see that her face was pale and her forehead glistened with a film of the kind of greasy, damp perspiration that comes with illness.

I didn't say anything about it. Hadley and I got the birds ready for the oven. A little salt and pepper. A strip of bacon over the breast of each bird. Put them on a rack in a roasting pan. And that was it.

With about fifteen minutes to go before the risotto was ready to come off, I put the roasting pan into the oven and started a saucepan of water for asparagus. To me, the aromas were sublime.

They made Marsha sick to her stomach.

"I've got to go lie down. Call me when you're ready to serve."

I did. And she tried, but she couldn't handle that dinner. We opened doors and windows to air out the cooking smells and Hadley and I sat down to a quiet supper. Everything was delicious. Hadley ate Marsha's woodcock. I insisted, saying I'd get more.

When we were doing the dishes, Hadley said, "Well, it was a great dinner, Dad, except for one thing."

Yes, I said, she had that right.

"I feel so bad about Mom. I wish we hadn't tried to cook that dinner."

"She wouldn't have allowed us not to. Don't worry; she'll be all right in the morning."

"Well," Hadley said, and I could see she was fighting tears, "it will be different next time. At Christmas—with those grouse. Don't you think so, Dad?"

"I'm sure of it."

We finished up in the kitchen and sat in front of the fire for a while. Hadley sat on the floor with Jeb and rubbed his back, which he appreciated and responded to with low, satisfied moans.

"You've got a kitchen, right?" I said, out of the blue. "In your apartment in Boston, I mean."

"Yes," Hadley said. "Why?"

"Well, why don't we go out for a little while in the morning? Just a couple of hours. We'll get another three birds. I'll clean them and send them back with you to school, in a cooler. You can make a woodcock dinner, like this one, for your roommates."

"Neat," Hadley said, and smiled for the first time in a couple of hours. "That'll be so cool. My roommates won't believe it."

"Let's do it, then. But we have to get started early. If you miss that bus, I'll have to drive you back to Boston, and I don't want to be away that long."

"Sure," Hadley said. Then she looked down at Jeb. "What about you, buddy—will you find us some more birds in the morning?"

Jeb wagged his tail as though to say, *No sweat. Consider it done.*

We had a plan and we went to bed on it.

I worried—as if I didn't have better things to worry about—that the woodcock might have moved on or that, for some reason, Jeb wouldn't be able to find them if they were still around. I should have been worried about something really important. Like, for instance, my shooting.

There were plenty of birds around and Jeb had no trouble finding them. But I couldn't hit anything . . . couldn't have hit the ocean if I was standing on the beach, in range and aiming at it. After half a dozen clean misses, I finally connected. Jeb retrieved the bird and dropped it at my feet. *Here,* he seemed to be saying, *this is what they look like. If I can find them, then the least you can do is hit them.*

"Maybe that will break my slump," I said.

"Yeah," Hadley said. "But don't we need to be going? It's getting kind of late."

We'd decided that, no matter what, we would quit hunting and start back for the house at ten. It was a quarter till.

"Just a few more minutes. We need two more birds."

Jeb found another and I got this one, too.

"One more."

"It's ten o'clock, Dad."

"Okay. We'll have to rush a little, but we'll make it."

By the time I got the third bird, it was past ten-thirty and we were in a genuine time squeeze. When we pulled into the garage at home, I said, "Okay, you shower and pack and I'll clean these birds. We've got half an hour."

"All right."

Hadley did her part, but when it came time to leave the house—right now or miss the bus—I still had one bird to go. I could have skinned it, instead of plucking it, but that just didn't seem right. I wanted my daughter's woodcock prepared the sovereign way.

"All right," I said. "You drive my truck. I'll sit on the passenger side and finish this bird on the way."

It was about a fifteen-minute ride to the bus stop. I pulled feathers the whole way and tried to stuff the ones I'd pulled into the mouth of a shopping bag that was open between my feet. About half the feathers made it into the bag. The other half were swirling around on the vagrant breezes inside the cab of my old truck. When we got to town, we got some looks from people in their cars when they pulled up next to us at the light. We must have looked like one of those itinerant families, traveling with the prize chickens.

I put the final carcass—expertly plucked—into a small cooler just about the same time Hadley parked at the bus stop and the big cruiser pulled up and opened its doors.

"Here you go, kid," I said. "Have a great dinner."

"Thanks, Dad," Hadley said, in a tone that said a lot more. Including, perhaps, "I can't believe you."

I watched the bus depart, then drove to the car wash and spent about twenty minutes and a pocketful of quarters vacuuming woodcock feathers out of the cab of my truck. I couldn't get them all, however, and for months afterwards, the occasional stray feather would start floating around the cab when I was driving somewhere, and my thoughts would go back to that day.

It was another story in the family fund and, as with so many of them, Jeb had a leading role.

There are a couple of postscripts to that story: First, Hadley spent a couple of hours in the kitchen of her small student apartment, making a meal around those three woodcock for her roommates. When she called home in the middle of the week, to check on her mother, I asked her how it had gone.

"Great," she said. "Everything was delicious. And all the dishes were ready at the same time. Well . . . almost. Only one problem, though."

"What's that?"

"My roommates couldn't stand the taste of woodcock."

"That's too bad," I said.

"Well, not really. They each took one bite. That meant I got to eat the rest. They were delicious. So thanks for plucking them. And thank Jeb, too."

I said I would, and when I did, Jeb wagged his tail like he understood entirely.

The other postscript . . . Marsha kept her promise and went out with us on opening day, the next season.

SEVENTEEN

For years, I had been hearing about the bird hunting in the West—Montana and Idaho, particularly—and the stories made it sound irresistible. You hunted big country, for one thing. Could walk all day long and never cut a road or cross a fence line. For Jeb, that would be paradise. According to the legends, the birds were plentiful, and challenging. I especially liked what I'd heard about sharptail grouse and Hungarian partridge. They both flew strong, and you could find them in cover heavy enough that they would hold for a point.

There was also the fact that you were hunting in that wide, lonesome region where you could drive for an hour between towns, and when you did find one, it would have one gas station, one restaurant and bar, and, maybe, one motel. So you could fill your gas tank, eat a steak, drink a beer, and get a decent night's sleep in a clean, cheap room. What more could you need?

Two or three times, I'd made tentative plans to go out West for the month of September with Jeb. Friends had offered to put me up and show me the ropes, even getting me on ranches where they had permission to hunt. I'd always had to cancel for one reason or another, including my wife's illness.

In 2001, it looked like I'd finally be able to follow through and spend the last two weeks of September in Montana and Saskatchewan. I was actually doing a little preliminary packing when I got a call and heard the words that were being spoken all across the country.

"Turn on your television."

Like everyone who watched that morning, I experienced a sudden clarity of perspective. Lots of things that had seemed almost urgently important the moment before I turned on the television and saw those two buildings burning—those things now seemed trivial and inconsequential.

Flying to Salt Lake and then driving to Montana for ten days of bird hunting now seemed like a fool's errand. There was only one destination that seemed worth the trip, and that was New York, to do whatever I could to help. Also, my daughter Brooke was there.

She'd been on her way to work from her apartment in Brooklyn when she looked up and saw the impact of the second plane when it flew into the South Tower. She went back to her apartment and, from the roof, watched the fires burn, the people jumping to avoid being burned alive, and, then, the buildings collapse.

She called on her cell phone. I said what I could to calm her down. Told her to go out and buy batteries and bottled water, and then we made plans for her to get out of New York and come to Vermont. It was a couple of tense days before she could take the Amtrak out of Penn Station to Albany.

We watched the broadcast of the memorial service, the president's visit to Ground Zero, and all the other coverage. The television became the nucleus of our lives and everything orbited around it.

And, then, after a few days, what had always been true now became clear. Life would go on. The office where Brooke worked reopened, and she caught a train down to the city and went back to work. The airports reopened—though with the terminals now patrolled by soldiers carrying M16s—and a few planes began to fly.

I still had a ticket to Salt Lake and a rental SUV waiting for me there. "Why don't you go?" my wife said.

"I don't know. I don't much feel like it. Doesn't seem right, somehow."

"Hanging around here watching television isn't really accomplishing anything," she pointed out.

"No. I guess not."

"We all have to just get on with our lives. When that changes, you'll know it. Until then, stick to the plan."

So I made a call out West to see if the friend I'd planned to meet up with was still game.

"Sure," he said. "People are going back to school, back to the mall."

"Then I'll see you in a couple of days." It was, as much as anything, a matter of not knowing what else to do.

The airport felt like a church on Saturday. Empty and quiet; almost hushed. I'd learned by now that Jeb needed a little help with his flying anxiety, so I'd gotten some tranquilizers from Jean Ceglowski. There was no howling this time when Jeb's crate went onto the conveyor belt and disappeared behind the wall.

We had the plane almost entirely to ourselves. The cabin attendants were exceedingly polite and the mood, everywhere, was fragile as glass. Everyone was still in the late stages of shock and trying not to think about what could happen when you were flying innocently between cities on an airliner.

It was still daylight when we landed at Salt Lake. I had about a ten-hour drive ahead of me. After a while, I'd left the city behind and was out in the open country. The desert felt very lonely. Jeb was in the back of the SUV, still in his crate, and sleeping. I pulled off at one of those interstate rest stops and let him out. He was still a little groggy from the drugs.

"Come on, bud. Why don't you ride up front with me."

He jumped up into the passenger seat and I was glad to have him there, even when he curled up and went back to sleep. There are times when the wordless companionship of a dog is just the thing, and this, surely, was one of them.

I got to the motel in the little Montana town a couple of hours after midnight. There was a key waiting for me at the office door with a note that said I could register in the morning. I was so tired I unloaded only the bag I needed, and Jeb, who was reluctant. He didn't know about this town, this room . . . this whole deal. But he knew (I'm guessing here) that I wasn't going anywhere unless it was in that nice blue Dodge Ram. So if he stayed in his crate, in the back of that SUV, he wasn't going to be left behind.

That's the best way I can account for why he refused to lie down on either the floor or the bed in that motel room. He paced and clawed at the door until I let him out. Then he trotted over to that Dodge Ram and clawed at the back gate until I unlocked it, opened it, and let him in. He jumped up into his crate and curled up on the frayed old blanket I'd put in there for his comfort. Then he sighed, content at last.

"Good night, bud," I said, and I heard the sound of his tail hitting the side of the crate.

I locked him in and went back to the room for a couple of hours of sleep.

I met my companion in the morning. Leigh Perkins, chairman of the Orvis company and a close friend, was one of the people who had been telling me about the wonderful bird hunting in the West, keeping after me to come out and try it.

"Good trip?" he asked.

"Quiet and uneventful," I replied.

"Those are good things," Leigh said.

We ate breakfast at a place where the regulars had their own coffee mugs hanging from pegs on the wall. They served those exceedingly ample breakfasts—four eggs with a side stack of pancakes and an order of bacon—and I remembered I hadn't eaten dinner the night before. I devoured one of the best short-order breakfasts I could remember eating. I drank two cups of coffee and sort of envied the people at the back of the room who were still smokers, enjoying a cigarette with that second cup.

After breakfast, we loaded Jeb and Leigh's two dogs, a setter named Dagmar and a Brittany named Val, into his SUV, and drove to a ranch where he had permission to hunt. It was what they think of as a "short drive" out West—sixty or seventy miles—and along the way, we passed a couple of those silos where the Minutemen missiles are poised and ready for Armageddon. I imagined that things had been fairly tense down in the control rooms over the last several days.

We visited with the ranchers who were friendly and cheerful, and seemed eager for us to sit and drink some coffee and talk. You can go days without visitors living out on the plains, and company is a treat. We stayed long enough to be polite, and could have hung around all morning.

We drove to the top of a wide mesa that had been planted in wheat and, since the cutting, was now covered with stubble. There was thick cover on the edges of the fields and steep coulees running down the face of the mesa. It looked ideal. The birds would feed on the edges of the wheat fields, then use the border areas and the grown-over coulees for cover.

We put two dogs on the ground. Leigh generously let Jeb have a slot in the first brace. It was still fairly early in the morning, the best time of day for finding birds, and his dogs had vastly more experience than Jeb. We'd have increased our odds by using his two dogs since they were much the better performers. But Leigh knew I had come a long way and he understood that I was a little nutty about my dog . . . and appreciated it, since he was that way, himself, about his own dogs.

Jeb and Dagmar worked all right together. Which is to say, they pretty much ignored each other. There was more than enough country for both of them to hunt, and they took advantage of this fact. I tried to keep an eye on Jeb and he did stay in view. But if he never tried to run away, that didn't mean he wasn't doing some big running. And enjoying every minute.

That morning set the tone for the rest of our week. We got into both sharptail and Huns. The dogs worked fine, and on a couple of occasions, one would point and the other would back. I remember one scene vividly. Dagmar and Jeb were on a small knob out in front of us. The knob was grown up in some kind of lush, tawny-colored grass that grew just short of knee-high. There were a few small ponderosa pines growing on the knob, and above us, surrounding everything, one of those dramatic Montana skies. Deeply blue and endless. There was something almost trancelike about the scene.

So it was startling when I realized that I was looking at two dogs, on point, up on the knob. I wasn't sure which dog had hit a point first. It looked like Jeb was backing Dagmar, but it could have been the other way around.

However it had come about, it was a striking picture. Those two small, sinuous dogs in the thick grass and scattered pines under that boundless blue sky. The kind of scene you realize, even as you are looking at it, that you will never forget.

They were pointing a big covey of Huns, and Leigh and I each got a bird on the covey rise. The dogs retrieved and then followed the singles down a coulee. We stayed on the lip of the coulee until we saw a point, then we'd push our way through the thick growth that included wild roses until a bird flushed and we got a shot. We picked up another four Huns before we turned around and headed back up to the flat of the mesa.

It was like that all day, and by late afternoon, when the air began to cool, we had plenty of birds. No limits, but close. And measuring a day by whether or not you get a limit is clear evidence of a pretty impoverished vision.

I know that I'd never had a better day in the field, and I think I can speak for Jeb on this matter and say that he hadn't, either.

Leigh and I ate good steaks at the local cowboy restaurant and bar, then spent the night in the same motel. Jeb had gotten over his fear of being left behind, and he stayed in the room with me. He started out on the floor, but it wasn't long before he was up on the bed with me. The motel owner had told Leigh that he didn't mind dogs staying in the rooms.

"They're a lot neater and cleaner than some of the other occupants," he said.

We covered a lot of ground that week. Spent one full day driving up into Saskatchewan to meet three young hunters who knew Leigh and had invited us up. The border crossing, in the wake of 9/11, was a long, drawn-out ordeal, especially with the shotguns we were carrying. We made it to the farmhouse the three men were renting long after dark, but still in time for dinner, which was sharptail grouse.

These men had come up from Virginia, by car, bringing their dogs with them. They were undeniably serious bird hunters, and I worried that Jeb and I might be a little out of our league.

But we held our own. Jeb made some points and never really embarrassed himself. He did kill one porcupine. It took us about half an hour to pull the quills, and when we were finished and trying to clean the blood off our hands, Jeb took off and started looking for birds—and porcupines—like nothing had happened.

"Stout dog," one of my hosts said.

"He never seems to learn," I said.

"Some never do. I had one like that. He was a good old dog—like that one of yours."

It was high praise, and I wore it for the rest of the day.

We hunted three days in Saskatchewan and then drove back through Montana, stopping at a couple of places on the way to Leigh's home in Wyoming. By the end of the week, Jeb had pointed—and I had shot—

sharptail grouse, Hungarian partridge, and sage grouse. I'd also done some duck shooting, which didn't include Jeb, and, of course, he had rid the world of that unholy porcupine. It had been a great week in spite of the pall that had been cast over everything by the attacks on 9/11. These were never too far out of my mind.

Leigh had an interesting story to tell about that. He'd been hunting with an old friend and they'd had a wonderful morning. He called back to the office to check on things, and was chatting up his assistant about this and that when she said, gently, "Leigh, do you have any idea what is going on?"

He didn't, so she told him.

"You can imagine how that changed the mood," Leigh said.

Still, we'd had a fine time, and there was something very satisfying about watching my dog work the big, unfamiliar country. I'd always admired his stamina and he showed plenty of that on this trip. I was also impressed with the way he quickly took to sleeping in motels. He might have been born knowing how to do it. He'd also showed himself to be a fine road companion. He could sleep for two hundred miles without a whimper. He didn't have any problem making himself comfortable, and if he needed to stop, he'd let us know in plenty of time.

"We need to do this again," I said to Jeb when we were waiting in the Salt Lake City airport for his crate to be checked and loaded, along with my duffel and shotguns. I'd given Jeb his tranquilizer so he was sitting at my feet, looking a little stunned. The people in line behind us probably thought I was the one on drugs, however. Talking to a dog like he was another human.

"Next time," I said, ignoring them, "we'll just drive the whole thing. I don't like the airplanes any more than you do, and even if it takes a little longer, it means you get to spend a couple of extra nights in a motel."

No sign that he understood what I was talking about, but it wasn't important since I was really just talking to myself. But I liked the sound of what I was saying. Neither Jeb nor I was getting any younger. Another long road trip—possibly even as good as this one had been—seemed like something to look forward to, and to plan and to dream about during the long months between the last day of the bird season back home and opening day out here in the West.

"We'll do it, bud," I said. "That's a promise."

When I put Jeb into his cage, the man behind me gave a look that said the wrong animal was in the box; I was the one who needed to be locked up.

EIGHTEEN

Throughout a disappointing bird season in Vermont, I thought—and dreamed—of the next trip Jeb and I would take out West. I imagined the two of us, driving down a long, empty section-road with grain fields as far as you could see and a single windmill on the horizon, turning monotonously. We would stay in cheap motels where they didn't mind dogs and eat at places where chicken-fried steak was the specialty. We would cover miles and miles of ground, on foot, looking for birds. And we would find enough of them to make it a hunt, and a memorable one.

When summer came around and bird season seemed less distant and theoretical, I got out the maps and I studied guidebooks and Web sites. I set my dates and called and e-mailed friends to warn them I was coming, and to ask them if they knew of places to hunt and, by the way, would they like to join me and Jeb for a day in the field? This way, I slowly put together an itinerary. I did this with some care; perhaps because I figured that this was probably the last time Jeb and I would make a trip like this. He was ten, old for a pointer, even if he still acted like a pup and still loved to see the ground rolling under his belly.

I was driving a small SUV, but there was still plenty of room, so I packed lavishly. A couple of side-by-sides—a 20- and a 28-gauge—and a few boxes of shells. Also two pairs of boots. Briarproof pants. Vest and waxed cotton jacket. Various hats, gloves, and the necessary number of shirts and socks. I packed a tent and sleeping bag. Cooking gear, camp stove, and ax. Miscellaneous odds and ends, to include a twenty-five-pound bag of dog food, a cooler for any birds I shot, and a couple of books on tape to help me through all those miles on the interstate.

We left early, just at sunrise, on a Sunday morning. It was raining and cold for October. But like everyone who has ever headed West, I was full of hope. We'd had such poor bird hunting in New England. Things had to be better out there.

We took I-80 and drove up through New York toward the Great Lakes. We caught the Cleveland rush hour and pushed on for Chicago, where Brooke who had left New York, was in graduate school. She had invited us to spend the night. She missed Jeb.

He rode complacently on top of my big duffel, sleeping most of the way. Now and then, he would come up front and sit with me for a while. I would stroke his neck and rub his ears. They were nicked and scarred, and one of them was missing a piece, at the tip, that was the size of a dime. Bitten out by another creature. A dog, probably, when he was off on a ramble.

I listened to a book on tape. A history of the making of the atomic bomb, by Richard Rhodes. It is a brilliant book and troubling, at its core. If this is the apex of the human enterprise, you think, then I believe I'll just head for the country and go bird hunting.

We stopped for gas when necessary, at a franchise place for lunch, and at the interstate rest stops when I thought Jeb needed a break. The miles seemed to melt away, and we crossed into the central time zone and gained an hour. Still, it was late when we pulled off the four-lane and started looking for Brooke's apartment on the south side of Chicago.

We found it, and she came down and helped me unpack the things I didn't want to leave in the SUV. The shotguns, especially. Then she rode with us and showed us the way to a garage where we could park overnight.

It was a walk of several blocks from the garage back to Brooke's apartment. And along the way, Jeb had to stop and mark just about every tree. College people have a lot of dogs, and Jeb had never before encountered so much scent. Fortunately, it was late, and we ran into only one or two dogs out with their owners for a walk. There was some growling and posturing, but nothing in the nature of a fight.

"You've never been to the city before, have you, buddy?" Brooke said. "It takes a little getting used to."

Jeb wagged his tail, sniffed another tree, and marked it.

He was fine when we got to Brooke's apartment. We visited for a while and had something to eat. Then Jeb found a corner and I got the sofa.

We still had a long way to go, so we were up and out early in the morning. Brooke walked with us to the garage on her way to the library, and then to class. I told her I'd let her know when we were coming back through and that we'd like to spend the night again if she would have us.

"I'd love it," she said. "I miss old Jeb."

"What about old Dad?"

"Him, too."

From Chicago, Jeb and I headed out across the great flat interior of the country. We crossed the Mississippi. Drove through the endless cornfields of Iowa and into Nebraska, and finally, after a full day of it, turned off the interstate onto a two-lane and headed north into the Sand Hill country. We still had three hours, or more, before we would arrive at our destination, which was Halsey. When I pulled up in front of the motel there, the odometer said that I had come 1,650 miles, and I figured that put me right about in the middle of America—both spiritually and geographically.

I checked in at the motel. Thirty-nine dollars a night. Ten dollars extra for the dog. Jeb and I took our walk. I put him in our motel room, then went across the street to the local bar and restaurant. There was a pool table just inside the front door, but what got your attention was the plastic figure of a woman crawling through what looked like an escape hatch in the ceiling. The usual beer signs and liquor bottles were on display behind the bar, where one stool was occupied by the man I was here to meet.

We shook, ordered drinks and dinner, and then he told me what he'd learned while he was waiting.

"I got the word on the national forest," Steve said. "Good sharptail and prairie chickens. But there's a hundred thousand acres, so it's going to take a lot of prospecting."

Which would be music to Jeb's ears, I thought.

"But then," Steve went on, "a little while ago, a fellow came in to pick up a couple of six-packs and we started talking. Turns out he has a seven-thousand-acre ranch, and the birds just love his irrigated alfalfa fields."

"Any chance of hunting them?"

"Done deal. I got directions. We can start there first thing in the morning."

There was snow on the ground and the sky was low and thick and the color of an old bruise when we met for breakfast.

"You hear the forecast?" I asked Steve.

"This front is supposed to blow through later this morning. Clear and cold behind it."

"How cold?"

"You'll need your jacket. And maybe a fleece to go under it."

We had one of those road breakfasts where cholesterol doesn't count. Eggs, sausage, home fries, biscuits. And coffee. Before we left, the waitress filled my old, dented thermos.

"Cold like this, you'll need it," she said.

We thanked her and left a large tip.

We followed the directions Steve had gotten the night before from the man whose farm we would be hunting. In a while we were off the blacktop and in four-wheel drive. There was still snow on the road but probably not enough to plow.

"We're looking for an alfalfa field," Steve said, "and one of those center-pivot irrigators."

We left the county road for a narrow little track through the hills. The slopes were grown up in short brown grass and there were windbreaks of cedar here and there.

"Are those trees native?" I asked. Steve was a Westerner; a photographer who got around and had the kind of curiosity you see a lot in sportsmen. They want to know about the country they are hunting; feel an obligation to be able to name the flora and fauna, and to understand how the land came to look the way it does.

"Planted," Steve said. "Ranchers did it to give their stock some protection from the wind. It blows all the time."

We found the alfalfa field, no problem. Our plan was to make a big circle around the edge and let Jeb work out ahead. He didn't know the country but didn't seem to mind. He ran with his customary exuberance, and Steve and I followed along. It felt good to be moving.

Twenty or thirty minutes after we started hunting, Jeb found birds in a little strip of corn planted on the edge of the alfalfa. A lot of birds; too many, in fact. More than fifty, anyway, and maybe a hundred. A lot of eyes. One pair of those eyes must have spotted Jeb on point and that bird flushed while we were still moving up. Then another two or three flew. And then, there were so many prairie chickens in the air that they looked like grasshoppers. I was just out of range and didn't shoot.

Jeb gave me a look. I read it as saying, *Man, if you'd only just hustled up here when I first pointed, you'd have been in range when they started flying. Even with that little 28-gauge.*

I apologized and said I'd be quicker next time.

I tried, but it didn't help. We saw a lot of birds and Jeb pointed some. But there were just too many of them. You don't often complain about too many birds, but that's what we were up against.

"Picture what it would have been like earlier in the season," Steve said. "When the birds were still scattered and you could find them in singles and pairs."

On another alfalfa field we put up three hundred birds, maybe more, and followed them into the cedar shelter belts. Now and then we would kick out a few sharptail, but mostly we saw chickens. And every one we saw was sixty yards out, or further. By lunch, I still had not fired a shot. But I had seen more birds in a morning, out here, than I'd flushed all season at home. Jeb might have been frustrated and a little exasperated with me. But I was having a fine time.

We checked in with the rancher who was stacking hay and seemed glad for a little company on a cold morning. He was wearing a quilted jumpsuit and a fur hat, and looked grateful for their warmth.

"Seen some?" he said.

"A lot. And always from a long way off."

He didn't seem surprised. We shared our sandwiches and coffee, and talked. He told us that his ranch, one of the oldest in the state, had been paid for by prairie chickens. Seems his great-grandfather shot them from a one-eyed horse with an old double-barrel gun that he could break and load quickly enough to get off four shots on the covey rise.

"Land went for a dollar an acre back then," the rancher said, "and restaurants in Kansas City would pay a dollar and a quarter for a chicken. He'd fill barrels with them. Salt them down and send them out."

Seven thousand acres' worth.

We talked about other things, and it occurred to me that this was one of the pleasures of hunting in the last few empty stretches of the country. It can get lonely, if you live there, and you appreciate the chance to visit with a stranger. It is harder and harder, all over the country, to get permission to hunt someone's land by just walking up and knocking on his door. But the more remote the country, the better your chances.

We all got cold after a while, so the rancher climbed into the heated cab of his tractor and went back to work. Steve and I went back to chasing chickens. The cold front had pushed the geese down and they flew over in long, watery V's, making their melancholy music. We saw an eagle, a bobcat, and a mule deer with a prodigious rack.

"Biggest I've ever seen," Steve said. "No question."

We saw more chickens, but at the end of the day, we hadn't shot enough to pay for a cup of coffee. Much less a seven-thousand-acre ranch.

Still, we ate and drank well that night, and decided to try the Nebraska National Forest in the morning. Maybe we'd do better on public land, we decided. Couldn't do any worse.

The next day, we drove by stands of twisted pines, introduced here by the Forest Service at the urging of Theodore Roosevelt, back when conservation meant not merely preserving wild land but improving it. The trees never panned out commercially, but the surviving stands provide habitat for deer and, especially, turkey.

We parked at a windmill and stock tank at the head of a long, treeless draw. We'd seen one grouse get out of a juniper on the way in, so we were optimistic. The native prairie grass was as thick as any on the private ranch, and there were sand cherries—the birds' favored food—on the north side of the ridgeline. By noon, we had covered a lot of promising ground without flushing any birds.

"Take you a month," Steve said.

"I'd settle for a week."

But I was due in Kansas that night to meet Ted Hatfield, Jeb's old friend. We had plans that included ducks, pheasants, and quail. The ranch with the alfalfa fields, where we'd hunted the day before, was on my way.

"Maybe we'll get lucky," I said.

We did. Jeb pointed and I made a long (read "lucky") shot, and we jumped a couple of mallards off a little pond when we snuck in, below the dam. Steve didn't eat prairie chickens, so I gave him the ducks, put the chicken in my cooler, and said good-bye. Then Jeb and I got back on the road. I left Nebraska feeling like it had been real good to me.

I drank coffee to stay awake and Jeb, who had run himself out on the ridgelines, slept soundly on top of my duffel in the back. We made almost four hundred miles in eight hours, and were only a few minutes late when we met Ted Hatfield at the Kansas City airport. By midnight, we'd found ourselves a cheap motel that would take dogs, but only in the smoking rooms. Jeb didn't smoke but he did like the room. We put in for a wake-up, and it came early.

We ate breakfast at a place called Quackers, in Mound City, Missouri. It was barely dark-thirty but the place was already half full. All the customers were dressed in some kind of camouflage ensemble, and the air was thick with bacon grease and cigarette smoke.

"You want coffee?" the waitress asked. That time of morning, it was a purely rhetorical question.

She was about eight months pregnant. The third man at our table, Fred, looked at her and said, "Well, I guess we know how you're spending your free time."

"I can't wait," the waitress said. "It'll be my fifth one."

"Sweetheart," Fred said, "you need to buy yourself a television."

We ordered the duck hunter's health-food breakfast—eggs over easy, sausage, potatoes, and buttered toast—sprinkled salt and steak sauce on top of everything, and ate like wolves, smearing up the last of the egg yolk and steak sauce with the last piece of toast.

An hour later, we were on a flooded field of corn and millet at the edge of the Squaw Creek Wildlife Preserve. There wasn't anything Jeb could do on a duck hunt and Fred had a Lab, named Bud, for retrieving. So we left Jeb in Fred's cabin, which was warmer and more comfortable than the SUV. Still, he howled when we left and walked across a levy to our blind. When we got there, at dawn, there were so many geese on the horizon, they could have been clouds. The mallards started coming in a little after sunrise, one and two at a time.

"It'll pick up later," Fred said, like he was apologizing.

He'd bought the property twenty years ago, he said, and he wouldn't sell now if someone offered him a thousand times what he'd paid for it. I wouldn't have been here except that Fred and Hatfield were old buddies. These days, it seems, some of the best hunting opportunities come through networking. I hadn't driven west with duck hunting in mind. But I wasn't going to turn down an invitation; especially not for something this good. Still, I did feel a little guilty over leaving Jeb. We were too far from the cabin for me to hear him if he was still howling, so I told myself he probably wasn't. And knew that was a lie. I told myself I would make it up to him on quail and pheasant, starting right after lunch.

The ducks came to calls and to the wing action of one of those motorized decoys, and we could hear the sound—like wind through branches—when they dropped from way out of gun range until they were right on top of us. When we'd shot our limits of mallards, Fred said, "Try some of those teal. For lagniappe."

By mid-morning, we were through shooting. Ducks, anyway.

It was opening weekend for pheasant in Kansas, and there was good public hunting for roosters out in the north-central part of the state on the Glen Elder Reservoir. But the duck shoot had taken longer than we'd thought, and there was the business of lunch at another short-order place. And, then, Ted had lined up a place in the Flint Hills where he thought we'd find some quail. There was more hunting than we had time for, and we needed to do some driving to get to the hunting. But that's what I'd come for—the driving and the hunting—so we thanked Fred for the duck hunting, and it was back on the road again.

"Let's pass on the pheasant," Ted said, "and go for the quail. Your bobwhite is the sovereign upland bird where dogs are concerned, so I'm sure that's what Jeb would want."

"Talked me right into it."

The next morning, we were in the Flint Hills of Kansas, on a private ranch, where we started at the top of a long draw that was grown up in some scrubby juniper and other trees and shrubs. On the flanks of the draw were acres and acres of dry, tawny prairie grass that seemed to go all the way to the horizon. Which was, approximately, how far Jeb ran on his first cast.

"He still likes to cover the country, doesn't he?" Ted said.

"Descendant of the legendary Guardrail," I said. "The ultimate big-going dog."

Once Jeb was done limbering up, we moved down the draw and quickly started finding birds. Jeb would be running flat out, then lock up, almost in mid-stride in that wonderful, purposeful pose of a bird dog on point. Ted and I would walk in and pass him and the birds would get up. We'd shoot the covey rise, then watch the singles spread out in the prairie grass. Jeb would retrieve what we had shot on the covey rise, then point a couple of the singles before I would call him off and we'd start back down the draw, looking for another covey. This was quail hunting as it was meant to be. We found five coveys in the first three hours.

Jeb did not kill any porcupines, run any deer, or bust any coveys. The only thing he did wrong all morning was point every pack-rat den he came on. He would leave most of them, after a minute or two. But occasionally, I had to go in and pull him off. This was bad form but, otherwise, I was proud of him. He was finding birds, pointing birds, and retrieving birds. And having a hell of a time.

"I believe he likes this road-trip business," I said. "I need to get him out more often."

That afternoon, after lunch, Jeb had pointed a covey and was working up the singles when he got diverted by another pack-rat nest. For some reason this one seemed especially compelling.

"I guess I'd better go in and get him."

I had just finished saying this when Jeb charged into the nest and came out with a skunk in his jaws. He got the whole treatment, on his face, down his neck, and in his throat and eyes. Parts of him were green. I picked up a little, myself, on my boots.

Well, these things happen when you are on the road. That, anyway, seemed to be Jeb's attitude. He didn't seem to think the fact that he was wearing essence of skunk was any reason to quit hunting. He thrashed around in the grass for a minute or two, then went back to work. Ten minutes after that, he was pointing a single. Proof that dogs have discriminating noses.

That night when we settled in, I scrubbed him with detergent, then with tomato juice. It did some good, but there was still a lingering fragrance of skunk about Jeb—almost an aura—and I made him sleep outside in his crate in the SUV. He was too rank to be inside the home that belonged to a friend of Ted's and where we were staying. I got a sullen greeting the next morning when I let him out and fed him. But his spirits picked up when we went back out in the field to hunt quail with Ted one more day. He made a couple of good points and there was something a little defiant about them. He was like the ballplayer who has been benched and when he gets back in, goes three for four just to show the manager what real talent looks like.

When we finished the hunt, I gave Jeb another bath and took one myself. Still, leaving Kansas for Iowa, we were a salty-looking—and smelling—outfit. There were feathers on the floor of my SUV and the upholstery was stained, here and there, with blood. My fifty-quart cooler was filled with a combination of mallards, teal, prairie chickens, and bobwhite quail. There were two pairs of muddy boots. A bag of dirty laundry. A couple of recently oiled shotguns. Some hamburger wrappers, empty paper cups, and shotgun shells. Also one tired dog, redolent of skunk and tomato juice. Hoping to keep the scent from impregnating the upholstery, I made him ride in his crate. Benched him again.

He gave me a look, as if to say, *Jeez, man. And with me on a hot streak.*

I thanked Ted for his hospitality.

"Wouldn't have missed it," he said. "That's quite a dog you've got there."

So Jeb and I got back on the road. By now, the highway was starting to feel like home, the way Merle Haggard sang it in "White Line Fever." There was something hypnotic about it, and I recalled an old friend who had spent five and a half years in the Hanoi Hilton as a prisoner of the North Vietnamese after the navy attack plane he was flying had been shot down.

"Motion is my mantra," Al Stafford had said to me. Once he got back to the U.S., Al had a hard time staying in one place, or even sitting still. The product, no doubt, of spending all those months in various cells, some so small that it was hard to lie down and stretch out to his full five foot ten inches. When he wasn't out in the Gulf of Mexico, single-handing his thirty-one-foot sloop, Al liked to drive up to Vermont from Pensacola, Florida, where he lived. And he enjoyed hunting with Jeb, perhaps because he sensed in him a soul mate.

"That dog likes to ramble almost as much as I do," Al said. "He needs a call sign. How about 'Wide Mover?' That ought to work."

My mind and memory drifted languidly to Al and other things as we rolled up another four hundred miles or so—me and Skunkman, aka Wide Mover—from Kansas up to Iowa City. It was Sunday, and we had a couple of football games to listen to on the radio. I turned up the volume so Jeb could hear in the back. The Chiefs were playing at home, and we ran into a bunch of their fans on the bypass around Kansas City. Lots of red cars and RVs, with all the appropriate decals and bumper stickers.

The Chiefs had won, so everyone was driving fast and with the confidence of Priest Holmes cutting off tackle and breaking into the clear.

It was late, almost midnight, when we got to Iowa City where a friend had found a motel that would take dogs. He hadn't mentioned the skunky part.

I hadn't seen Stan in, oh, three or four years. And if there wasn't any other point to this road trip, it was worth it just to see him. After a while, the e-mails and the telephone calls don't seem sufficient. Also, Stan had a baby girl whose adventures he had been chronicling, and I'd been looking forward to meeting her.

But Daisy had already left the house for kindergarten when I picked Stan up in the morning. We drove twenty minutes or so and met a half dozen of his friends who were waiting for us on the edge of a twenty-acre CRP field. It was supposed to be loaded with pheasant, and looked it.

We did the introductions, then got on line and started moving. Jeb had never hunted with so many people, and he wasn't sure of the drill. And he sure didn't understand why nobody shot at the hen pheasant that he put up almost right away.

"That's okay, man," I said. "Hunt 'em up."

It was one of those cold, raw days with the sky hanging low and dark all the way to the horizon. No green anywhere, and a sense of winter coming remorselessly on. It felt good to be walking, and our little skirmish line made good time across the field. I missed an easy, if slightly long, shot at a rooster. Then one got up close, between me and Stan, and we both shot. We called it a company bird.

By lunch there were only four of us left. The others had to get back to the office or the classroom, and their leaving was a sort of wake-up call for me. I had been on the road for more than a week now, and still had today and tomorrow to hunt. I'd been on a kind of sabbatical from the routine, and now it seemed almost normal to be spending my days on the highway or walking through a field somewhere behind a skunky dog. I wondered, idly, how long I could do it before it would get old, and decided that, for sure, I would never find out.

Stan and I took Jeb into a ten-acre island of willows and other brush in the middle of a large field of recently harvested corn. We'd heard roosters calling from inside the island, and Jeb worked with a kind of cool, resolute professionalism. He'd been on the road long enough now that this was routine stuff. Pure business. He pointed three hens before a rooster got up, and I dropped it with the second barrel.

Jeb brought the bird back at me in a way that said, *Piece of cake, Boss. Piece of cake.*

"You the man," I said to him. "Now find one for Stan."

He did. And by the time the rain started, we were all ready to quit. It had been a good day. That night, Stan and his wife had Jeb and me over for dinner. Daisy loved Jeb, and didn't seem to notice the skunk smell. We had one of those evenings of catching up that you can have with old friends, when the conversation is somehow both comfortable and fresh.

When we checked out of the motel the next morning and loaded up, I said to Jeb, "Well, buddy, this is it. Last lap. After this, it's home for the winter."

He gave me a look and I'd swear that he got it.

We hunted a mix of private and public land, and it seemed like somebody might have been there before us. Jeb made a couple of tentative points but nothing got up. Late in the morning, we flushed a single hen and she was out of gun range. The day warmed and the dog began to lope through the cover like he didn't have a lot of confidence in this program but, since it was his job, he'd put in an honest day's work.

We ate some sandwiches and sardines for lunch. Talked about maybe bagging it early.

"If I started home now," I said, "I might make it to Cleveland tonight. Be an easier drive for me tomorrow."

"Makes sense," Stan said.

"But, then, I'd just spend the winter thinking about how I'd quit early when I was in the tenderloin of Iowa pheasant country with time to hunt. I've got enough regrets already."

So, we hunted one last piece of ground. Jeb ran ahead, quartering efficiently, and I followed, trying to concentrate on the scene so that it would be indelibly printed in my memory. The bare, skeletal trees against the putty-colored sky. The dog moving along the edge of the recently harvested cornfield. The distant formation of geese. So it was even more of a surprise than usual when the covey of quail got up.

We managed to mark them down. Jeb did some good work on the singles, and that seemed like the right finishing note. So with plenty of daylight left in the day, I gave Stan some quail and one of the mallards from the nearly full cooler, thanked him, and promised to stay in touch. Jeb settled into his crate and I started down the section-road, and then the two-lane that took me to the interstate.

I had a cooler full of ducks, pheasant, quail, sharptail grouse, and prairie chickens. And a weary dog whose ribs showed and who smelled like a skunk. My vehicle needed a good cleaning, inside and out. I was tired and filled with gratitude.

The road is some kind of righteous therapy, I thought, whether you need it or not.

"That was a fine trip, General Stuart," I said. It seemed appropriate to speak formally to Jeb and to use his rank. He'd earned it. With the exception of the skunk episode, he'd been an ace, and I wrote that off as being part of that wild, ungovernable side of him that would never go away, and that, in fact, I didn't want him to lose.

I called Brooke from the highway and told her that we wouldn't be stopping by to spend the night.

"I'm disappointed," she said.

"Yeah, but you'd be really unhappy living in an apartment that smelled like a skunk."

"Oh," she said. "So, what's the deal? He couldn't find any porcupines?"

"Something like that."

"Well, trust old Jeb to improvise," Brooke said. "I'm sorry you won't be stopping, but I definitely won't insist. You two drive safely."

"We will," I said. Thinking, what's with the *we* business?

"And give Jeb a hug for me, will you, Dad?"

"In a week or two, maybe."

When I'd finished the call, I spoke over my shoulder to Jeb. "Brooke says hi, and she's sorry you won't be dropping by."

He wagged his tail so I could hear it thumping the side of the crate.

NINETEEN

The trip ended when we pulled into my driveway, late one cold, clear night after almost five thousand miles on the road. Jeb and I had hunted in four states. I was tired but happy. Jeb smelled like a skunk and he was happy, too . . . possibly *because* he smelled like a skunk.

We both slept long and well.

In the morning, I gave him a bath in hot, soapy water and rubbed him down with a solution of baking soda and hydrogen peroxide to cut the smell. And it worked . . . a little.

I unloaded the SUV and spent the day oiling guns, cleaning boots, washing clothes, storing gear, and plucking birds. Jeb followed me around and watched me while I worked. It occurred to me when I had finished all these chores that this trip had been that rare thing—something that had lived up, completely, to my expectations.

"Maybe we'll do it again next year," I said to Jeb. "What do you think?"

Judging by his body language, he thought it was a fine idea.

And why not? We had proved we were a good team. We might not have been as young and nimble as we once were, but we could still cover the necessary ground. If we'd lost a step or two, we were also smarter than we had been. We were now a couple of old veterans who made up in guile for the physical gifts we'd lost.

I started thinking about the itinerary for our next trip.

But, then, when we'd been home for a couple of weeks, Jeb started to cough. Actually, he'd been doing a little of it ever since we'd started on our way back. I'd put it down to the skunk, which he'd had firmly in his mouth, so some of the spray had to have gone straight down his windpipe. I would have been coughing, too, I thought. And probably a lot worse than Jeb.

"It sounds really bad," my wife said, after one of Jeb's coughing fits.

"Just a reaction to the skunk," I said.

"Then why does it keep getting worse?"

"I dunno," I said sagely.

"Well, I think you ought to get Jean to look at him."

"He'll be all right. And if he isn't in another week or two, I'll take him out there."

The cough got worse. And worse. And as it got worse, Jeb seemed to decline almost in front of our eyes. He didn't have his old energy or his customary appetite. He coughed so hard, sometimes, it seemed like he might crack a rib. He couldn't sleep and, increasingly, neither could we.

"You know," Marsha said one morning, "you really . . . "

"I know," I said. "I'll call Jean and take him out there today."

Jean Ceglowski had never seen Jeb looking so depleted and dispirited.

"Oh, my," she said to him. "You don't look at all well. Let's get you up on the table and find out what the problem is."

Which was easier said than done. She couldn't find anything in her office exam, so she took blood and sent it out to a lab for a workup. But that didn't produce any answers. She put him on antibiotics, but when the prescription ran out, he wasn't any better. Was worse, in fact. He spent most of the day on his bed and got up, it seemed, only to cough. And the coughing had become deeper and the spells lasted longer. When they were over, he would lie down, exhausted and plainly in pain.

Jean suspected some kind of congestive heart condition which, to me, carried a sound of finality.

"Is there anything we can do?"

"I won't know without getting a look at his heart."

"How do you do that?"

"With ultrasound," she said, and explained that she would have to bring in another vet, who had the equipment and training, to do the test. Depending on what it showed, there might be some remedies, including surgery, for Jeb's condition.

The test, she explained gently, wasn't cheap. And the surgery would be even more expensive.

"Well, let's do the test," I said. "Then, we'll see."

I carried Jeb out of her office since he was almost too weak to walk. He had lost weight and felt pitifully light. I looked up at the long ridgeline, bare and gray in the early days of winter, before the first snow. Jeb and I had hunted up there a lot, and he'd found plenty of birds. It hadn't been very good the few times we'd tried it this season, and I wondered if we'd ever hunt there again. I was beginning to think we wouldn't.

I wondered if, perhaps, the next time I brought Jeb out here, it would be so Jean could give him the final shot that would put him down and out of what had plainly become misery.

I thought about this on the drive home, telling myself that it had been a good run and this was some consolation. Jeb was ten years old and it had been a very full decade. We'd ranged pretty wide and had ourselves some very good times. We'd made a lot of deposits in that memory fund of mine.

When I was back home, I carried Jeb inside and put him on his bed, in front of the woodstove. He looked up at me and, with my instinct for anthropomorphization, I saw in his face a blend of gratitude and a plea to please do something.

Come on, Boss Man. Don't give up on me. I ain't dead, yet.

"We'll get that heart test done, bud," I said. "Maybe that will tell us something. But you know what?"

He gave me that look of curiosity. Like he truly was waiting for an explanation.

"Whatever is ailing you, I don't believe there's anything wrong with your heart. That's the strongest part of you."

Which turned out to be true. I took him back in for the ultrasound and watched as Jean and the other vet administered the test. You could see a kind of watery display of Jeb's chest on a liquid crystal screen. It was large—but not enlarged—and even my untrained eye could see that it was not merely healthy but robust. It beat with authority, and the valves moved in a kind of sturdy, reliable rhythm you'd hope for in your car's V-8.

"I know a lot of men my age who'd like to have a heart that looked like that," I said.

"I'm sure," Jean said. "Well, at least we know what it *isn't*."

Once again, I carried Jeb out to the truck and put him in the passenger seat. I had another supply of antibiotics. And some steroids—Jean thought they were worth a try. Meanwhile, she said, she would make some calls to the school of veterinary medicine at Cornell. It was one of the best in the country and she was a graduate. Maybe someone over there would have an idea.

I drove home in gloom.

I was thinking a lot these days about Jeb, and feeling a kind of depressed, premature nostalgia for all the good times we'd had. It seemed remarkable in some way that this dog should mean so much to me, and I suppose it was inevitable that I should start asking myself . . . why? He was, after all, a dog, and I had never been one of those people who mistake the affections of an animal for the love of a child. He wasn't my baby and never had been. He was my dog. I'd never lost sight of that distinction.

There had never been much chance I would go to the other extreme and consider Jeb as mere livestock, the way some of the men I'd known, back when I was a boy, had viewed their pointers. I'd been put off by their coldness and borderline cruelty, even back then, and now I saw it as not only emotionally repellent but also kind of pointless. I mean, if you couldn't feel some affection for your dog, after he'd beaten himself bloody in a briar patch hunting for birds for you to shoot . . . well, then, what was the point. Give it up and hunt deer. The better to take out your cold superiority on lesser mammals.

I *liked* dogs—and pointers, especially—even before my girls made me a gift of Jeb Stuart. I just hadn't expected ever to feel as much for a dog as I did for this one. Nor would I have ever expected to be as certain as I was that these feelings were requited, unconditionally.

But I did, in spite of the sophisticated thinking—based in evolutionary biology—that characterizes dogs as nature's most highly evolved con men. According to this line of thought, all those things that we sentimental humans take as demonstrations of love and loyalty are, in fact, learned behaviors and hardwired into the genes. Dogs, from the time the first cavemen let them get close to the fire, have been manipulating humans for handouts, shelter, and protection. You can buy a lot of those things, dogs learned, by licking some faces and wagging your tail and otherwise acting as though you think some human is just the finest specimen in all creation. Make a human think you love him, and he'll do just about anything for you.

The way this theory has it, dogs may be trained by their masters, in a rudimentary sort of way; but masters are manipulated by their dogs in a way that is complete and so subtle that the masters think they are acting out of their own free will.

I didn't buy that, either, but not because I had any better logic to explain dog behavior or why humans find it so beguiling. But, to me, the evolutionary explanation seemed just too cold and too easy—almost tautological. Animals do what they do because they do what works. And what works is what they do. And so forth.

There is a certain elegant symmetry to the argument, but it doesn't—to my mind, anyway—hold up. For one thing, there are too many hard cases that are exceptions. Most of them on the human side, but some on the animal. Certain individual humans in some cultures—and some entire cultures—are not softened up by the affectionate displays of dogs, and treat them cruelly. There are more than enough dog-haters to be merely statistical exceptions to the rule. And, a few antisocial dogs as well.

And, then, there is something pretty guileless and fairly excessive about dogs. Cats insinuate themselves among humans with a lot less effort. Dogs, as so many stories have proved, will go the last mile for a beloved master. Stories of dogs on the battlefield, staying near their masters' bodies in spite of shell fire. There is a Newfoundland buried somewhere on the battlefield of Antietam who would not leave his dead master even in the worst of the fighting, and was eventually killed by artillery himself. You have to strain logic to find an evolutionary payoff in that behavior.

And, anyway, after a while, it begins to feel like a profitless game, trying to account for the behavior of dogs by citing Darwin, or even E. O. Wilson, of whom I am a great admirer.

If the evolutionists want to find pure, rational, unsentimental, biological antecedents for Jeb Stuart's behavior, then I say . . . "Have at it, boys. Me and Jeb are going hunting."

They can argue that Jeb doesn't *really* feel any great affection or loyalty for me. He merely carries the genetic knowledge of how I will react if he does those things that make me think he feels that way. Namely, that I'll feed him and give him a warm place to sleep.

If this is so, then Jeb has certainly found other, incentiveless reasons for doing what he can to make me feel good. When I blew an artery inside my head and had to spend time in bed, recovering, Jeb would not leave my side. He followed me when I hobbled into the bathroom, and if I drifted off, when I opened my eyes I would see Jeb, six inches away, staring into my face to make sure I was going to wake up. My wife tells me that when I am on the road, he checks my office three or four times a day, and sleeps there at night, if she'll let him.

There was a bond, then, between Jeb and me, and I believed it went beyond simple, tactical self-interest. Now, he was dying.

I didn't know what to do, except to try to make him comfortable. I kept the fire going in the woodstove. Fed him the pills from Jean Ce-glowski until the prescription had run out. I talked to him when we were in the same room and rubbed his ears and his brisket, which he seemed to appreciate. It may even have given him some relief; the pain in his chest had to have been intense.

Since I couldn't think of anything else to do, and nothing Jean had tried so far seemed to work, I got on the phone and called around to bird hunters I knew. I'd tell them about Jeb's condition and ask if they'd ever heard of anything like it.

Inevitably, the answer would come back: "No. Sorry." Or some-thing like that.

I had more or less given up hope and was imagining that last trip out to see Jean when I got a callback from one of my hunting acquain-tances. He'd been traveling when I first called and I'd left a message.

"Sorry I didn't get back to you sooner," he said. "Finding any birds? How's old Jeb? Keeping the porcupines honest?"

Jeb, I said, wasn't hunting porcupines, or anything else, these days.

"What's the problem?"

I explained.

"You know," the man said, "a friend of mine from around here went out West with his setter and the same thing happened. He came back and the dog started coughing. He thought the dog was done for."

"But the dog made it?"

"Yeah. Some kind of special vetting did the trick. I don't remember the story, but I can give you the guy's number."

"Please," I said.

I called the number immediately. The man who owned the setter was at work. I spoke to his wife.

"Yes," she said, "that dog was real sick. I don't remember exactly who he went to and what medicines it took, but the dog is fine now."

I asked her if she would give her husband my number and ask him to call me.

"Of course," she said. "And don't worry about your dog. My husband thought he was going to lose that setter of his, and he's crazy about that dog. But the dog is fine now."

"Thank you," I said, and settled into an impatient wait for her husband's return call.

He must have appreciated my anxiety. The phone rang shortly after five.

"My wife told me about your dog," he said. "Sounds like the same thing mine went through."

It was a seed, he explained, from a plant that he'd heard called "cheat grass."

"It's not a native plant," he said. "The way I understand, it came in on sheep, from Spain. But what happens is, the dog breathes in that seed when he is running through the grass. It gets down in the lungs, and because it has these little, almost microscopic barbs on it, the seed attaches itself to the lining of the lungs where it causes swelling and makes the dog cough. Infections set in. Lots of dogs die from it."

"What," I asked, "can you do?"

"First couple of vets I went to didn't know. Then, I found one who had heard about this problem and prescribed heavy—no, massive—doses of antibiotics and steroids. It took a while but the dog got better. He's fine now."

I asked him for the name and number of the vet and thanked him extravagantly for his help.

"No problem," he said. "I sure hope it works out for your dog."

When I called Jean, she said, "I was just about to give you a call. I've been talking to someone over at Cornell . . . "

Turned out she'd heard the same diagnosis and the treatment from someone she'd talked to over there.

"Why don't you bring Jeb out and we'll get him started with those medications right away."

It took most of the spring for Jeb to recover, and there were days when we couldn't be sure that he was making any progress at all. I studied him for signs. Tried to gauge how much he was coughing one day as compared to the one before, and the previous week. I monitored his appetite and his weight. When he got back to eating his normal rations, I felt like celebrating.

"What about a walk, old buddy?" I said.

Jeb took me up on it. We went up into the woods and he was tentative, at first, staying at my heel. But after a few minutes, the old urges took over and he started to run. It wasn't the old Jeb. Not yet, anyway. But I could see the familiar form in the way he moved, and what I felt at that moment was more than simple relief. It was a kind of gratitude and, indeed, joy. He had crossed some kind of threshold, and we'd been given a reprieve.

We'd had a great run, and it wasn't over yet.

Jeb made a complete recovery. We didn't make another road trip that fall, but that was all right. I was completely content to hunt around home and, even, not to hunt at all. We didn't find many birds, but that was fine. We still had evenings in front of the fire and walks in the woods. Jeb was still running, and even if it wasn't with his old style and endurance, it was a pleasure to watch.

I now had a new dilemma to brood over. Even with the reprieve, Jeb was coming to the end of the line. I knew I should be thinking about a pup, but I couldn't bring myself to even consider it. The thing with Jeb had been too good, and I couldn't get my mind around the idea of another dog taking his place.

Then, one afternoon, Hadley—who was married, now, and living in a town a few miles up the road from us—dropped by to visit.

"Guess what?" she said.

I told her I couldn't guess. But I assumed it was good news—she looked happy.

"I bought a dog."

"You've already got a dog."

"Yeah. But not like this dog."

"How so?"

"This one is a pointer. And not just any old pointer, either. I bought a Guardrail Pointer. A female. But she looks just like Jeb. Same identical markings. I'm picking her up at the airport in two weeks."

"That's great," I said, skeptically. None knew better than I what a handful a pointer pup could be. But then, Hadley had the skills with dogs that I'd always lacked.

"Guess what I'm going to name her, Dad?" Hadley said. She was so enthusiastic, it was clear my skepticism hadn't registered.

"Tell me."

"Dixie," Hadley said proudly. "On her papers, she'll be 'The Dixie Flier.'"

"Wonderful."

"And we'll take her out together."

"For sure."

"Will you help me train her?"

"Absolutely," I said. "I would be honored."

And so, it was starting all over again, with a puppy and a whole decade of accumulating memories to look forward to.

Already, I couldn't wait.

CODA

Jeb is now twelve, and if he's slowed down, it isn't by much. He has become the only dog in a house where there had always been at least two, and as many as twelve. (Hadley's Lab Tickle once had a litter of ten, which made for interesting times.) Jeb has moved into a kind of elder-statesman role, and in recognition of his seniority, and long and (mostly) faithful service, we began pampering him in small ways. We added real meat to his normal dry-food rations. Bought him more comfortable dog beds. Tolerated his sleeping on the living room couch. He's been indulged, then, and has reciprocated in his own small ways. It has been two years, now, since he nailed a porcupine.

Hadley lives about twenty miles away with her pointer, Dixie. It is summer, as I write, with the bird season still more than two months off, but already I am eager and curious to see how Dixie will do in the field. She has all the moves, which she demonstrates by pointing grasshoppers and songbirds when Hadley drops by to visit and brings her along. Jeb does not deign to join her in the grasshopper hunts. Those days are behind him. He prefers to lie on the grass and smell the flowers . . . among other things.

Marsha passed through her medical crisis and is talking about going out with me when I take Jeb and Dixie into the field. Brooke has moved

195

on with her life and, as I write, is overseas. She e-mails frequently and always asks to be remembered to Jeb.

Jeb's twelfth birthday came around last week. What, I asked myself, is the proper gift for a dog who has everything and has brought so much to the party for so long. I gave him some hamburger and took him on a four-mile run. He stayed with me the whole way and did not find any manure piles to roll in.

Later that afternoon, I went out to cut the grass and Jeb went with me. He roamed the edge of the meadow, beyond the lawn, checking for scent. I kept a wary eye on him, knowing that he hadn't used up all his energy on our run and still had enough in the tank for a jailbreak.

I'd had my back to him for a while, and when I turned I couldn't see him.

"Same old Jeb," I thought, and shut down the mower. I walked to the last place I'd seen him and called, "Jeb. Here."

Nothing.

He'd done it again, I thought. Probably just for old time's sake and to show me there was still life in those old bones. I walked a few more steps, into the tree line, and I saw him. He was on point and it was serious. This was no chipmunk or robin.

I walked in a few more steps and a grouse flushed, flying as though it were injured and, perhaps, had a broken wing. It was the dodge that mother birds use when their young are near. She was trying to draw danger away from her brood.

I called to Jeb. I didn't want to disturb any young grouse and make them show themselves. There were hawks around. Plenty of them. I was pretty sure I'd seen a goshawk, a couple of days earlier, in a stand of pines on the edge of my property. A goshawk would make short work of young grouse.

Jeb took one step and the young birds began coming out of the underbrush. They didn't fly with the drive and purpose of mature birds, but they could get around.

"Come on, Jeb," I said. "Let's go finish the yard work. We'll find more, just like them, in a couple of months."

He'd followed the flight of the young birds and marked them down. In the old days, there would have been no way of persuading him to leave them. But he was older now, and wiser.

He followed me back into the yard.

"I don't know about you, buddy," I said, "but I can't wait for October."

He gave me a look and wagged his tail, and it was unmistakable what he was trying to say.

Neither can I, Boss Man. Neither can I.